ISAAC NEWTON
ORGANIZING THE UNIVERSE

ISAAC NEWTON
ORGANIZING THE UNIVERSE

William J. Boerst

MORGAN
REYNOLDS
Publishing, Inc.

620 South Elm Street, Suite 223
Greensboro, North Carolina 27406
http://www.morganreynolds.com

RENAISSANCE SCIENTISTS

Nicholas Copernicus

Tycho Brahe

Johannes Kepler

Galileo Galilei

Isaac Newton

ISAAC NEWTON: ORGANIZING THE UNIVERSE

Library of Congress Cataloging-in-Publication Data

Boerst, William J.
  Isaac Newton : organizing the universe / William J. Boerst.
      p. cm. — (Renaissance scientists)
  Summary: Presents the life and work of the famous seventeenth-century
  British physicist.
  Includes bibliographical references and index.
    ISBN 1-931798-01-X (lib. bdg.)
    1. Newton, Isaac, Sir, 1642-1727—Juvenile literature. 2.
  Physicists—Great Britain—Biography—Juvenile literature. [1. Newton,
  Isaac, Sir, 1642-1727. 2. Physicists. 3. Scientists.] I. Title. II.
  Series.
    QC16.N7B54 2004
    530'.092—dc22

                    2003014571

Printed in the United States of America
First Edition

CONTENTS

Portrait of Sir Isaac Newton by Godfrey Kneller. *(Courtesy of Erich Lessing / Art Resource.)*

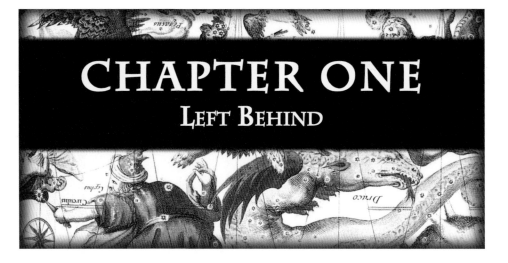

CHAPTER ONE
LEFT BEHIND

Shortly before his death, Isaac Newton commented to a friend: "I do not know what I may seem to the world, but, as to myself, I seem to have been only like a boy playing on the seashore, and diverting myself in now and then finding a smoother pebble or a prettier shell than ordinary, whilst the great ocean of truth lay all undiscovered before me." These modest words reveal Newton's genius for seeing the underlying simplicity in what most of us view as nature's nearly overwhelming complexity.

Ironically, there is no record of Newton ever walking on the seashore, either as a boy or as a man. His life was spent in three principal locations: Lincolnshire, the county of his birth in east central England; Cambridge;

and London. But from this relatively tiny portion of Earth, he was able to explain that the same force holding our solar system together also made the seas rush to— and from—the shore, and fruit fall to the ground. Not only did he visualize the invisible, he developed the mathematical tools necessary to measure the fundamental physical forces of nature.

Isaac Newton, maybe the greatest scientific mind ever to live, was not supposed to survive his first day. When he was born prematurely on Christmas Day, 1642 he was so small his mother said there was not enough of him to fill a quart pot. He later recounted that he had been "so little likely to live that when two women were sent to Lady Pakenham at North Witham for something for him they sate down on a stile by the way and said there was no occasion for making haste for they were sure the child would be dead before they could get back." He surprised everyone by surviving, although for months he was too weak to hold his head upright and had to have a special collar made to steady his neck.

The circumstances of Newton's birth were taxing to Hannah Newton for another reason. The boy's father, also named Isaac, had died just a few months earlier, in October. The tiny newborn was their first child.

The fact that he had arrived early, on Christmas, had cheated death, and was a posthumous child, gave Isaac a deep conviction that he had a special purpose in life. As an adult, Newton was extremely confident of his abilities. He had little patience for those who doubted

Seventeenth Century England

Isaac Newton spent his life in Lincolnshire county, Cambridge, and London.

that he was right about the physics of motion and force, or how gravity worked, or what light was made of.

When Newton was three he was dealt another blow when his mother remarried, in January 1646. The Rector of North Witham, Barnabas Smith, was a wealthy man whose wife had died the previous June. Smith was sixty-three and had no desire to bring the boy to live at the rectory. Isaac had to stay with his maternal grandparents, the Ayscoughs, at Woolsthorpe, the manor Hannah had inherited from his father. As part of the marriage arrangements, Hannah insisted that Smith give her son a piece of property and remodel the Woolsthorpe manor.

After his mother left Woolsthorpe, Isaac was lonely. Sometimes he could be seen swaying at the top of a tree, gazing southward across the mile and a half to the steeple of the church at North Witham where his mother lived with her new husband. These early years, separated from his mother, fatherless before he was even born, and left in the care of two elderly relatives who apparently did not have deep feelings for the boy, left emotional scars. In later life, Newton never discussed his grandmother, not even remarking to anyone when she died. As for his grandfather, Isaac was excluded from his will, which suggests their relationship was not a close one.

The Newtons had been settled in the area for centuries. One ancestor from the sixteenth century, John Newton, had purchased a farm of more than one hundred acres, including sixty acres of arable land. His son

Richard, Isaac's great-grandfather, had farmed the land. The family house, which stood on an acre or two of level ground, was two stories high with a stone barn attached to one side. Because the soil was too poor to produce much in the way of crops, most of the family's income came from selling sheep's wool. Isaac's great-grandfather, Richard, had seven children, two who died during childbirth or due to childhood illness. Isaac's grandfather, Robert, was born around 1570, and he eventually added a manor to the family estate. Robert had eleven children, of whom only six survived into adulthood.

During his childhood, Isaac had two uncles and three aunts who lived nearby with their children. Isaac never bonded with any of his cousins. Whether this was the result of his early experiences, or because his genius set him so far away from them, Isaac Newton had a very isolated childhood.

Rector Smith lived for eight years after marrying Isaac's mother. He died at age seventy-one, in August of 1653. During her marriage to Smith, Hannah gave birth to three children, Benjamin, Mary, and Hannah. After her husband's death, Hannah and her new children returned to Woolsthorpe, and Isaac. Both Mary and young Hannah were under two years old at the time, and surely kept Isaac's mother very busy. Her firstborn, deserted for eight years, now had to compete with his younger half-siblings for his mother's attention.

Later in life, Isaac kept notebooks that reveal the anger he felt towards his mother and stepfather, as well as the influence of Puritan religion on his upbringing. In a private, coded shorthand, he recorded his sincere attempts to atone by listing his sins. One entry mentions sinful deeds: "Threatening my father and mother Smith to burne them and the house over them" and "Wishing death and hoping it to some."

During Newton's childhood, England was in the middle of the conflict now called the English Civil War, a complicated struggle between opposing religious groups as well as between differing political philosophies. The war began the year Isaac was born. The two principal leaders of the conflict were Oliver Cromwell and King Charles I. Cromwell was a Puritan, and the leader of the forces fighting against the autocratic king and his Royalist supporters. Charles was defeated on the battlefield, captured, and beheaded in 1649. Cromwell assumed power and ruled until his death in 1658. The monarchy was restored under King Charles II in 1660 and England entered a period known as the Restoration.

Isaac lived with his mother and half-siblings at Woolsthorpe for almost two years, until 1654, when he left to attend King's School in the

Oliver Cromwell was a key figure in the English Civil War. *(Courtesy of Victoria and Albert Museum, London / Art Resource.)*

nearby village of Granth-am. The boy's intelligence was obvious. Although Newton's father had been illiterate, Hannah wanted Isaac to enter the ranks of the educated.

King's School was 130 years old in 1654. The school had an excellent reputation. It had a tradition of educating area boys in Latin, Greek, and the other subjects that made up the typical curriculum. Because most of the students would grow up to be

An English classroom scene from the seventeenth century. *(From J. Komensky, "Orbis Sensualium Pictus".)*

farmers and merchants, they were also taught practical mathematics, which was unusual for English schools of the time. As an adult, Newton was fluent in Latin, the primary language for scholarship.

Grantham was seven miles from Woolsthorpe, too far for the boy to travel each day. It was arranged that he would stay with the Clark family who lived near the school. Mr. Clark was an apothecary, or chemist (what we would call a pharmacist) and the family lived above the apothecary shop. Mr. Clark's wife had three children from a previous marriage who went by their biological father's name of Storer.

Isaac shared a bedroom with the two sons, Arthur and Edward. He did not get along with his roommates. On the way to school one day, Arthur kicked him in the stomach. Isaac challenged him to a fight and won.

In addition to his formal education, Isaac read the books from his stepfather's library, which he had inherited. He pored over John Bate's *The Mysteries of Nature and Art*. From instructions in Bate's book, Isaac constructed a small cart propelled by a hand crank that he could sit in and ride. He also built a small paper lantern that he would carry to school on dark mornings. When he arrived, he simply extinguished the light, folded it up, and put it in his pocket. Newton learned how to construct kites, as well. One story is that he placed his lantern on the tail of a kite and flew it at night to frighten the townspeople who could not identify the strange object. He also experimented with stringing the kites in different ways to achieve the most lift from the wind.

Besides learning through independent reading and school, Newton learned from his own observations. When a windmill was constructed north of Grantham, he watched as it was being built. Then he constructed a model version. He also made toys, and doll furniture, for Mr. Clark's stepdaughter and her friends. He got along well with the younger girl. If there ever any romance between them, it was the first and last time Isaac Newton was involved in any romantic entanglements.

In these days before accurate clocks the sundial was still the most common method of telling time. Isaac built sundials all around the Clark family apartment. Eventually, the entire Clark family, as well as their neighbors, were using "Isaac's dials" to keep track of the time. He became such an expert at sundial building that later in life he could tell the time of day merely by glancing at the angles of the shadows in the room.

Another fortuitous aspect of Isaac's time at Grantham

HISTORY OF SUNDIALS

The first instrument for measuring time dates back to around 3500 B.C., and was likely a simple pole placed in the ground. The pole cast a shadow that, as it shifted, could be used to measure the passage of time. By the eighth century B.C., slightly more precise instruments had been developed. The earliest surviving example of a sundial is from Egypt and is from around this time. It was made of stone and consisted of a flat base with six time divisions etched into it and a raised crosspiece at one end. The stone would be placed with the crosspiece in one position (east) for the morning and in the opposite position (west) for the afternoon. The shadow of the crosspiece would move across the six marked divisions to display the time. The Greeks and Romans refined the crude sundial, using their geometrical knowledge to add complexity and precision to the instrument. Later, the Arabs would use trigonometry to make the timepiece even more accurate.

More advanced sundials divided the period of daylight into twelve units of time. As the length of the day varied with the changing of the seasons, so did the duration of the time units. This variation was more noticeable in the northern and southern regions of the globe than it was in parts of the world nearer the Equator.

The development of sundials quickened in Europe during the Renaissance, and designs became more intricate to allow for more information, such as minute and hour marks and calendar dates, to appear. By the early modern era it was possible to build a sundial that could be accurate to within a minute, and when the first mechanical clocks came into use, sundials were used to check their accuracy.

was his exposure to Mr. Clark's apothecary shop. It was probably here that Isaac first spied into the world of chemistry. Mr. Clark's mixing of cures and potions appealed to the boy's curious and creative nature. He did some of his own experiments with items from the shop. His journals from the time have prescriptions for making paints, cutting glass, and creating baits for fishing. One recipe was for healing surgical cuts to the body: "Drinking twice or thrice a day ¼ mint and wormwood and 300 millipedes well beaten (when their heads are pulled off) in a mortar ¼ & suspended in 4 gallons of ale in its fermentation."

Isaac also became a clever sketch artist and displayed his drawings on the walls in the bedroom he shared. He made detailed drawings of ships, plants, birds, animals, and people, including portraits of the poet John Donne, King Charles I, and his schoolmaster, Mr. Stokes. This skill, too, served him later when he made sketches of his experiments to illustrate his scientific insights.

Mr. Stokes was a positive influence on Isaac. He rebuked the boy when he fell behind in his studies because he was spending too much time building windmills and sundials. Isaac would apply himself to his schoolwork, but then his attention would be distracted by some other intellectual curiosity and he would fall behind again. Eventually, Isaac learned to be more consistent in his studies and finished at the top of his class.

It was during this period, as Newton later said, that he performed his first experiment. It was 1658, the year

Oliver Cromwell died, and a great storm swept across England that became the stuff of legends for years. Isaac wanted to measure the force of the wind. He went out into the storm and jumped into the air with the wind, and then jumped against the wind. He marked how much the wind impeded or enabled his movement. He also claimed that he later used this new understanding of the wind's force to win a jumping contest with some of the local boys.

Depending on his mind instead of physical prowess to win an athletic contest did not endear Isaac to his schoolmates. Newton's aloofness tended to put off his fellow students and many of the townspeople, too. That he had the time to master so many skills and to build so many sundials is an indication of how much time he spent alone. Newton also had a problem controlling his temper. Like many children of the era, he was encouraged to keep a record of his "sins" and shortcomings. A few of his recordings reveal conflicts with other children: "Stealing cherry cobs from Eduard Storer," and then, "Denying that I did so." He expressed his "Peevishness at Master Clark for a piece of bread and butter," and confessed to "Putting a pin in John Keys hat on Thy day to pick [prick] him."

In 1659, the year Isaac turned seventeen, his mother decided that he had had enough education. She felt it was time for him to return home to learn how to run the family farm. Isaac returned to Woolsthorpe manor to live with his mother and three stepsiblings. The arrangement was troubled from the beginning. Newton continued to itemize his role in the domestic disputes:

> Refusing to go to the close at my mother's command.
> Striking many.
> Peevishness with my mother.
> With my sister.
> Punching my sister.
> Falling out with servants.

Newton had a tendency to get sidetracked from his chores by books and model building, and this also created trouble. As a farmer he was more of a liability than an asset. He let his farm work slide as he busily observed the world around him. He studied the movement of water in a stream while his sheep trampled a neighbor's crops. The local government twice fined him "for suffering his swine to trespass in the corn fields" and "for suffering his fence belonging to his yards to be out of repair."

This illustration depicts a typical seventeenth century farmworker in England.

Stories began to circulate about the strange Newton boy. One story told of Isaac leading a horse up a steep hill as he read a book. The horse slipped out of its bridle, and Isaac, oblivious of the escape, walked home dragging the empty bridle while the horse found its own way home.

Household servants soon concluded that he was a "foolish and lazy" boy.

Hannah decided to have a servant teach and supervise Isaac in his chores. But he duped the servant into doing the work himself while the young scholar-without-a-school sneaked away and catalogued a book collection recently left to Mr. Clark. Frustrated and at her wits' end, Hannah did not know what to do with her wayward son. Her dreams were centered around him building the farm into a profitable business. As she began to despair, Henry Stokes and Reverend William Ayscough (Hannah's brother) begged the stubborn Hannah to let the boy return to school. Mr. Stokes even offered to refund the forty shillings tuition. The men recognized Isaac's genius and argued that it was foolish to waste his talents shoveling manure, planting barley, and shearing sheep. Hannah eventually relented and in the fall of 1660 Isaac was back at King's School in Grantham.

Newton turned eighteen at the end of 1660. The following spring he was ready to leave for the university. Before he left, Mr. Stokes asked him to come stand beside him at the front of the classroom while he made a speech admonishing the other boys to emulate Isaac's accomplishments. The schoolmaster became so emotional there were tears in his eyes. Then the much-admired but still friendless student departed for Trinity College, at Cambridge University, in June of 1661.

CHAPTER TWO
TRINITY

Isaac Newton arrived in Cambridge on June 4, 1661, and enrolled at Trinity College the next day. Cambridge University, which was to be his home for most of the next forty years, was a collection of colleges. Trinity was one of the most famous, but Isaac's decision to go there probably had more to do with family connections than with its fame. The Reverend William Ayscough, Hannah's brother, was an alumnus. Humphrey Babington, another Trinity man, also sponsored Isaac. Babington was the brother of Mrs. Clark and a fellow, or member of the faculty. In fact, Babington was a senior fellow who held considerable political clout.

The Civil War in England had recently ended. Oliver Cromwell was dead, and the Stuarts had been restored to the throne. Charles II, son of the executed king, was the new ruler. The Restoration period began as those who had favored the crown during the long conflict, the Royalists, were restored to important positions. The College of the Holy and Undivided Trinity had been established by Henry VIII in 1546, after he had broken from the Roman Catholic Church over issues of divorce and property. Henry replaced the Catholic Church with the state-sanctioned Church of England, also known as the Anglican Church. Prior to the English civil war, during the reigns of Elizabeth I (1558-1603) and James I (1603-25), Trinity provided more bishops to the Anglican faith than any college in either Cambridge or Oxford, the other major English university. By the time Isaac entered in 1661, there were more than four hundred people, including students, professors, servants, and various other employees, at Trinity.

In order to gain admission, Isaac had to sit for examinations by the senior dean and the head lecturer who were charged with ensuring that incoming students met the entrance requirements. He had no difficulty gaining immediate admission. He kept a record of all his expenses; his first purchases included ink and a bottle to contain it, a notebook, candles, a desk lock, and a chamber pot.

Isaac entered Trinity as a subsizar, a student who helped to pay for his education by tending to the needs of the wealthier students. Among the duties of a subsizar were rousing upperclassmen for morning chapel, clean-

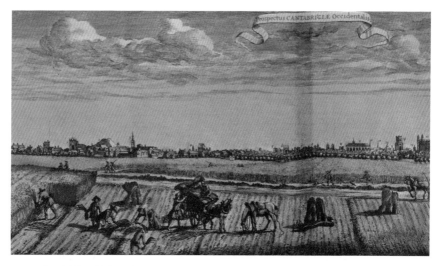

Cambridge University, viewed from across the western fields in the 1650s.

ing their boots, combing their hair, carrying meal orders to cooks, and waiting on tables. In chapel, subsizars sat in a place set off from the others. One historian described the subsizar as "a social pariah with whom men of ordinary good sense and good feeling hardly cared to be seen walking and conversing in public." The experience was made more painful because, at nineteen, Newton was two years older than most first-year students.

While money might have been tight, the main reason Isaac had to work as a subsizar was his mother's miserly ways. The university expenses came to around fifteen pounds per year, plus approximately ten pounds for personal needs. Hannah could have easily afforded that amount. She had an income of about seven hundred pounds per year from the estate of Reverend Smith. Apparently, she was still not convinced that a university education was the best route for her son. To her mind, land was the only thing of real value. All she would provide Isaac was the ten pounds personal allowance. Isaac, however, soon found a way to supplement his income. He became a moneylender, loaning students sums at a set rate of interest. He also added to his income by taking other students' turns at standing watch in the hall—a duty expected of each student—for pay.

The university that Isaac entered was still officially committed to the curriculum that had dominated European universities since the fourteenth century. This curriculum was based on the philosophy of Aristotle, the ancient Greek scholar who had written about a wide variety of subjects, including literature, politics and science. Together, these subjects were referred to as Natural Philosophy until the nineteenth century. Aristotle had developed a philosophy that incorporated astronomy and terrestrial physics into a unified, comprehensive world system. A stationary Earth was at the center of the orbits of the five known planets, the Moon, and the Sun. The finite universe was enclosed in an outer sphere of

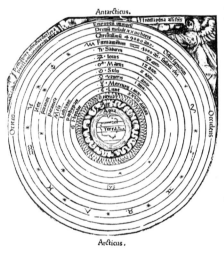

Aristotle developed a model of the universe made up of nested spheres, in which the planets orbited a central Earth. *(From Aristotle: Libri de caelo. IIII. Edited by Johann Eck, Augsburg, 1519.)*

stars. From the Moon out to the starry sphere everything was composed of a single, immutable element called aether. The sublunar sphere, which included Earth, was composed of four elements—earth, wind, fire, and water. Motion itself was either circular, which was considered natural and perfect; or linear; or violent, the motion that resulted from an impetus.

By 1661, when Isaac entered Trinity, the work of Nicholas Copernicus, Johannes Kepler, and Galileo Galilei had poked so many holes in Aristotelian physics and astronomy that few serious natural philosophers supported them any longer. The administrators and professors were slower to change, and the universities were still officially dedicated to Aristotle.

Copernicus's 1543 book, *On the Revolutions of the Celestial Spheres,* made the surprising argument that

the Sun, and not Earth, was located at the center of the revolving planets. According to Copernicus, Earth occupied the third position of the six known planets, orbited the Sun once a year, and rotated on its axis once a day. He supported his radical new planetary model with page after page of mathematical and geometrical calculations.

Nicholas Copernicus. *(Courtesy of the District Museum, Torun.)*

COPERNICUS AND TYCHO

In 1610, Galileo Galilei discovered that Venus cycled through phases similar to those of Earth's satellite.

This was impossible in the geocentric model designed by Claudius Ptolemy, which was based on the ideas of Aristotle. However, the phases of Venus did not prove that Copernicus's heliostatic model was correct, either. There was an alternative. Danish astronomer Tycho Brahe had devised a composite system in which all the planets, except Earth, revolved around the Sun, which in turn orbited a central, stationary Earth. Tycho's system was geometrically interchangeable with that of Copernicus, but did not require a moving Earth, which Tycho and many others thought was physically impossible.

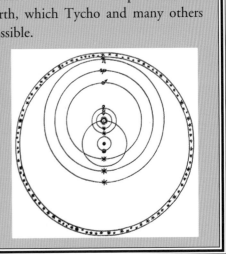

In this illustration of Tycho's system, Earth is the central figure. The small figure orbiting Earth is the Moon. The Sun resides three figures above Earth and moves in a circular path around it, and the rest of the planets rotate around the Sun. (From Tycho Brahe: Astronomiae Instauratae Mechanica, 1598. Courtesy of The Royal Library, Copenhagen.)

The German scientist Johannes Kepler (1571-1630) was one scientist who accepted Copernicus's Sun-centered, or heliocentric, premise. He went on to discover that the planets traveled in elliptical, rather than circular, orbits and that the speed of a planet's orbit varied relative to its distance from the Sun. Kepler also determined that there was a proportional relationship between the period, or duration, of a planet's orbit and its mean distance from the Sun. His work would be critical to Newton's later discoveries.

When Italian scholar Galileo Galilei (1564-1642) was tried for heresy in 1632 by the Roman Inquisition for his public advocacy of the Copernican model of the universe, the effects reverberated throughout Europe. In addition to stressing the developing rift between science and religion, the trial popularized the work of both Galileo and Copernicus. Beyond the specifics of the conflict was the growing belief that natural philosophers should be allowed to study nature without preconceived ideas.

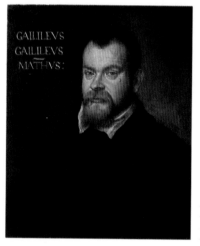

For Newton, the less-than-cutting-edge university system might have had its benefits. It was not particularly challenging, which left him plenty of free time to improve his Latin and broaden his knowledge of Greek and Hebrew. He spent most of his time on his own reading, primarily in the works of the more recent mathematicians and natural philosophers. The two most important of these were Galileo and the Frenchman René Descartes (1596-1650).

Galileo Galilei's work had a great influence on Newton as he developed his own theories of the universe through observation and calculation. *(Courtesy of the National Maritime Museum, London.)*

Galileo had become famous for his work in astronomy and the conflict it caused with the Catholic Church. In 1609 he turned a newly invented telescope to the heavens and discovered that the Moon's surface was not smooth and perfect as Aristotle had said, but craggy and rough. He also discovered that Jupiter had satellites and that Venus went through phases that would be impossible to explain if the planet were not orbiting the Sun. These observations were the first physical evidence that supported Copernicus's theory.

JUPITER'S MOONS

Galileo Galilei first revealed his discovery of four of Jupiter's moons in a pamphlet entitled "The Starry Messenger" that was published on March 13, 1610. The little book became a sensation. It made Galileo the most famous scientist in Europe, and set him on the path that eventually led to a public conflict with the Catholic Church over the religious implications of heliocentrism.

Galileo's work in physics, however, was equally important to the development of modern science. He rejected Aristotle's emphasis on common sense and perception, instead stressing the importance of mathematical quantification. When he began to question Aristotle's theory that heavy objects fell faster than lighter ones, Galileo did not merely formulate an elaborate argument based on speculation. Instead, he carefully measured the time it took a ball to roll down an incline and discovered a mathematical relationship between time and distance.

He used the experimental method to determine that Aristotle was wrong to say there were two distinct types of motion. Aristotle also said that the four elements were constantly striving to return to a state of rest. Galileo experimented until he concluded that an object would continue in its current state, whether that was a state of rest or a state of motion, until another force operated on it. Inertia, according to Galileo, referred to an object's current state without making reference to what the object was naturally inclined to do. Newton would later expand on this groundbreaking concept.

René Descartes is perhaps most famous for having said, *"Cogito ergo sum."* I think, therefore I am. *(Portrait by Franz Hals. Courtesy of Museé du Louvre.)*

Before Galileo, scientists had followed Aristotle's model of making an observation and then formulating laws to explain the observation. Galileo rejected this method, and deliberately tried to free his mind of what should happen in order to focus on what did happen. From the time of his earliest experiments, Newton adopted Galileo as a model of how a natural philosopher should work.

Newton read René Descartes's *Geometria* while at

Cambridge. In this work the Frenchman applied a coordinate system to the flat plane of the Euclidean geometry Newton had learned in school. This allowed for the assigning of numerical values to physical places. Pairs of numbers could be assigned to any location on the coordinate system. Space could be understood, and manipulated, by the use of algebraic symbols. Descartes moved geometry into a level of abstraction that made it possible to create formulas.

In his writing on physics, Descartes developed a theory to account for one of the most puzzling questions of his time. Scientists who rejected Aristotle's closed world system could not explain what force held the universe together and kept the planets moving in their orbits. Aristotle had said that the outer, starry sphere turned on its own, which in turn set the next inner sphere in motion. But if the universe was not contained

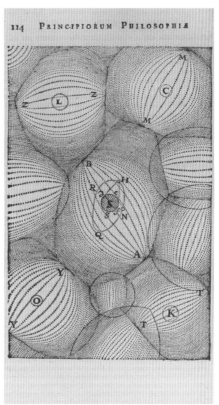

Descartes explained the universe as an intricate system of vortices, interlinked and in constant motion. Here, Descartes's vortices carry the planets around the sun. *(From Principia Philosophiae, 1644.)*

33 ※

in a system of interlocking spheres, what kept it from flying apart as the planets journeyed around the Sun?

Johannes Kepler had thought the force of the Sun propelled the planets, like a giant, invisible broom. Descartes, though, rejected any theory of force that did not have a physical explanation. He could not accept the idea of an invisible force, either attractive or propulsive, working throughout the universe. He thought the universe was a whirlpool of matter in motion. The Sun, each planet, and all other celestial bodies existed within a material vortex. This system of interconnected vortices was Descartes's organizing principal of the universe. Newton's greatest achievement would be to substitute gravitation for Descartes's vortices as the controlling force in the universe.

Descartes's material philosophy was popular when Newton was a student. Other mechanical philosophers working around the same time as Descartes were Pierre Gassendi in France and Thomas Hobbes in England. Newton read widely in the works of these thinkers. As a young man, he was particularly intrigued with Gassendi, who grounded his philosophy on the existence of tiny particles called atoms.

Descartes had a great influence on Newton in more abstract ways. The French philosopher maintained that because our senses cannot be trusted, we cannot be certain that the external world exists as our senses perceive it. This meant we could not depend on the information we gathered from our senses, as Aristotle

had believed we could do, but had to base our understanding of nature on mathematical quantification.

Early in 1663, Isaac skipped a dozen pages ahead in
his notebook and wrote across the top of a new page,
in Latin, "*Questiones quaedam philosophicae,*" or "Some
philosophical questions." Then he added, "I am a friend
of Plato, I am a friend of Aristotle, but truth is my greater
friend," alluding to a famous comment Aristotle made
when he dissented from Plato's teachings centuries
earlier. Newton then listed topics for further investigation. Among the headings were "Of Water and Salt,"
"Attraction Magnetical," "Of the Sun Stars and Planets
and Comets," and "Of Gravity and Levity." This list
grew from twelve entries to twenty-two then to forty-
five, and it marks the beginning of Newton's original
thinking on the natural world. From the very beginning
of his scientific investigations, he searched for truth
with little regard for precedence.

Newton's childhood experiences in isolation served
him well. He had few distractions from his work. In all
of his time at Trinity, he made only one real friend. He
had little respect for the other students, most of whom
were aristocrats who would eventually inherit land and
property or would have a well-paying position arranged
for them that would require very little work in return. His
one friend was John Wickins, who was equally bored by
the people around him. Wickins was the son of the
headmaster at Manchester Grammar School. The two
men remained friends for two decades. Wickins some-

times served as Isaac's assistant and secretary. He kept notes, set up experiments, and monitored investigations. Years later, well into the next century, Wickins's son recalled his father's account of meeting Isaac:

> My Father's Intimacy with Him came by mere accident My Father's first Chamber-fellow being very disagreeable to him, he retired one day into the Walks, where he found Mr. Newton solitary and dejected; Upon entering into discourse they found their cause of Retirement the same, & thereupon agreed to shake off their present disorderly Companions & Chum together, which they did as soon as conveniently they could, and so continued as long as my Father staid at College.

The fact that his college peers were not academically motivated actually worked to Isaac's advantage because it lowered the standards for promotion. Isaac could ignore his official studies for long periods of time and read and study what he wanted. When examination times came, he hurriedly read the required course material. Clearly, Newton's official studies did not overly challenge him. He easily passed his exams in 1664 and was promoted to the status of scholar. He was no longer a subsizar, but was now a full member of the university. He would receive a small stipend and a livery allowance. He was also assured of another four years of study at Trinity.

CHAPTER THREE
ANNUS MIRABILIS

By the spring of 1665, as he was finishing his under-graduate education, Isaac Newton had a firm under-standing of the scientific and mathematical discoveries that had been made over the preceding two centuries. His study of mathematics had led him from Euclid to Descartes, and his readings in science had introduced him to the works of Copernicus, Kepler, and Galileo. Over the next few decades Newton would synthesize the work of those who had come before him, add his own insights, and in the process create a system that would define the workings of the universe until new discov-eries finally forced alterations three hundred years later.

At the heart of many of the sixteenth century's developments in science and mathematics was a concern with motion and force. Copernicus had visualized a planetary system in which Earth orbited the Sun while also spinning on its axis—though he never could explain what propelled this motion, or what held the spinning universe together. Galileo's work with falling bodies and projectiles had placed the experimental method at the core of scientific research. Kepler had focused on the planets' paths around the Sun, proving their orbits were elliptical, and that the speed of the orbit varied depending on a planet's relative distance from the Sun.

Even before he entered Trinity College, Newton was committed to the scientific method advocated by Galileo with its emphasis on experimentation. He also agreed with him that nature was written in mathematics and only those who understood this language would be able to learn its secrets. Galileo wrote that hypotheses should be developed mathematically, tested in experiments, and the results then analyzed mathematically. Mathematics was both the instrument and the language of this new science. It was the tool used to formulate theories and the language used to communicate them.

The most important recent advancement in mathematics was Descartes's *Geometria*, which laid a coordinate system on Euclid's flat plane. The coordinate system could be used to assign numerical values to specific locations, which allowed for physical space to be understood abstractly. This made it possible to determine unknown values and to find the relationship between fixed points. But the science of the last hundred years was increasingly concerned with objects in constant yet varying motion. Descartes's geometry was inadequate for determining acceleration—the rate of change in a moving object's speed. Neither could it measure how a moving object's path would be altered by a change in speed. A new mathematics capable of measuring two quantities in constant flux was needed before natural philosophers could fully understand and describe motion, force, and gravity.

Newton wrote his first major mathematical paper in the spring of 1665. It dealt with ways to sum infinite series, a complicated concept involving a sum made up of an infinite number of terms. Soon after finishing it

In 1665, Newton attempted to solve for the area beneath this hyperbola. He took the calculation as far as he could, fifty-five places. *(Courtesy of Cambridge University.)*

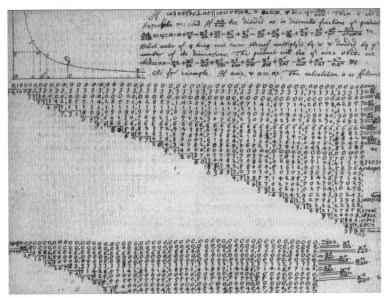

he planned another paper on a new, more complex problem: that of measuring the fluctuations of quantities subject to constant rates of change. But before he could begin this new work he had to leave Cambridge and return to Woolsthorpe.

In the summer of 1665, two French sailors had been found dead in London. After an investigation it was determined they had died of the dreaded bubonic plague, also known as the Black Death, which had killed one-third of Europe's population in the fifteenth century. This time around, the plague would take one hundred thousand English lives.

During the plague, doctors wore masks such as this one to protect themselves from the deadly disease.

The community of Cambridge did not suffer as much as the rest of England, but with its buildings crowded together along filthy streets it was a perfect breeding ground for the rats that carried the disease. In September 1665, the city cancelled a fair and stopped all public meetings; by October, all sermons and other gatherings were discontinued. That same month the university decided to close its doors and send everyone away until the plague had run its course.

Isaac remained in Woolsthorpe for the next two years.

A scene from the Great Plague of 1665. As graveyards overflowed, large pits were dug to bury the thousands of dead.

Isolated in the country, he was free to focus his mind and energy on the topics he had become fascinated with at the end of his undergraduate years at Cambridge. He was entering the most remarkably productive period in his life. Historians of science have come to call this period in young Newton's life *annus mirabilis*, the year of miracles.

During his first months back in Woolsthorpe, Newton turned his attention to continuing the work in mathematics he had begun the previous spring. He later turned his attention to optics, or the study of light, and conducted the experiments that would first bring him to the attention of the Royal Society, the organization of England's greatest scientists. He also began the speculations on motion and gravitation that he would return to periodically for many years.

Newton later wrote that during these months he "was in the prime of my age of invention and minded mathematics and philosophy more than any time since." He began by developing a form of mathematics powerful enough to deal with variations in two constantly varying quantities. He called his method fluxions—today we call it calculus. A monumental step forward, calculus made it possible to develop coordinates of distance and time and to derive expressions that designated speed, velocity and acceleration. Whereas Kepler and Galileo had been limited to finding definite values, calculus made it possible to consider quantities and values that were constantly changing, whether involving a projectile moving across Earth's surface, or a planet speeding around the Sun.

Other mathematicians were working, or had worked, on similar methods but no one had yet brought their ideas together into a coherent whole. Newton generalized his methods so that they could apply to a wide-ranging set of problems. Today most scholars consider him to be the first to develop calculus; however, he kept this discovery to himself for years. This characteristic hesitancy to reveal his work to the world would lead to one of the bitterest intellectual disputes of Newton's life when the German Gottfried Wilhelm von Liebniz claimed to have invented calculus first.

As startling as his discovery in mathematics was, Newton actually devoted more of his time in Woolsthorpe to studying optics, or the nature of light. It was during his sojourn away from Cambridge that Newton began to use his mechanical skills to design and build his own instruments for measuring light and to perform experi-

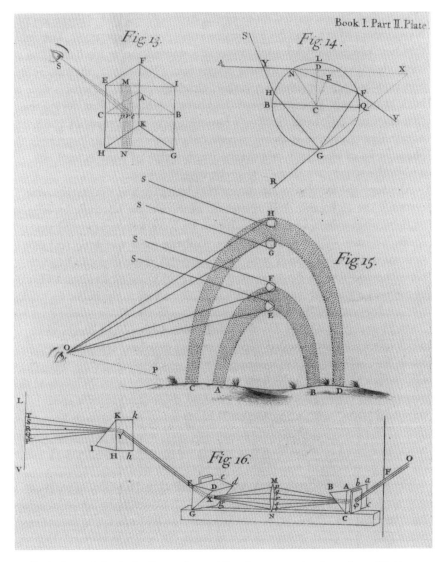

Illustrations of Newton's discoveries and theories concerning the nature of light and color, from his 1704 book, *Opticks*. This work built upon and refined the light experiments he performed during his *Annus Mirabilis*.

ments with them. He ground his own lenses for his optical experiments, which were primarily concerned with studying how light changed as it passed through a prism. Newton would write several papers on light theory for the Royal Society, which would culminate many years later with the publication of his work, *Opticks*.

The experiments Newton performed at this time were some of his most dangerous, and they demonstrate the extremes to which he was willing to go in his quest for understanding. For instance, in one experiment Newton deliberately stared at the sun's reflection in a mirror for as long as he could stand:

> I looked a very little while upon the Sun in a looking glass with my right eye and then turned my eyes into a dark corner of my chamber and winked to observe the impression made and the circles of colours which encompassed it and how they decayed by degrees and at last vanished. And now in a few hours' time I had brought my eyes to such a pass that I could look upon no bright object but I saw the Sun before me, so that I could neither write nor read but to recover the use of my eyes shut myself up in my chamber made dark for three days together and used all means to direct my imagination from the Sun.

Newton, like many other scientists, used his own body to make observations. His fascination with how light and sight worked is shown in this experiment:

> I took a bodkin [small dagger similar to a letter opener], and put it between my eye and the bone as near to the backside of my eye as I could: and pressing my eye with the end of it (so as to make the curvature

in my eye) there appeared several white, dark and coloured circles. Which circles were plainest when I continued to rub my eye with the point of the bodkin, but if I held my eye and the bodkin still though I continued to press my eye with it yet the circles would grow faint often disappear until I resumed them by moving my eye or the bodkin.

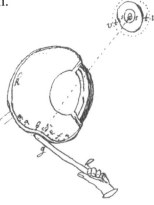

Newton's own illustration of his experiment using a bodkin to study the intricacies of light and its effect on the human eye. *(From Newton's manuscripts. Courtesy of Cambridge University.)*

Newton's keen and careful observations led him to his most famous discovery. There are many variations of the falling-apple story, some more fable than truth. In April of 1726, a year before he died, Newton first told the story of how a falling apple had influenced his thinking to Dr. William Stukeley, his first biographer. Stukeley wrote that after he and Newton had finished dinner they sat in the garden drinking tea under the shade of apple trees. "Amidst other discourse," Stukeley reports, "he told me, he was just in the same situation . . . when the notion of gravitation came into his mind. It was occasioned by the fall of the apple, as he sat in a contemplative mood."

While the details of the story may vary, we do know

that a falling apple set Newton onto the path that eventually led to his Law of Gravitation. Seeing the apple fall led Newton to think about why the force of Earth's gravity did not seem to decrease with distance. If the apple fell from a small tree, or from the tallest mountain, it would descend to Earth with the same force. Before Newton, people believed that gravity was a propulsive force—that it pushed objects away. Newton's observation of the apple suspending downward from the tree and then falling to the earth made him wonder if gravity wasn't in fact an attractive force that operated on every object in the universe. If so, Newton would be able to explain the relationship between Earth and the Moon, the very same relationship as that of the falling apple and the ground.

Galileo's motion studies convinced Newton that an object remained in motion, or at rest, until another force operated on it. Newton extended Galileo's law of inertia beyond Earth. A projectile sent into space would remain in motion until another force, in this case gravity, acted upon it. If the object were projected with enough force, Newton wondered, would it then enter into an orbit around Earth, similar to the Moon's? It would be years before he developed this basic idea into the central thesis of the Newtonian system—if Earth's gravitational pull held the Moon in its orbit, then all celestial bodies exerted, and were subject to, the same force.

At age twenty-four, Newton had begun the work toward making a conceptual breakthrough on gravitation that would eventually allow him to organize the universe into a coherent system. As he began to struggle with the mathematics involved with proving his theory, however, he ran into great difficulty. After weeks of struggle he threw the work down. The math simply was not up to his needs. Newton would eventually have to invent the math he needed. It would be years before he finally concluded his work on gravitation and published it in his great book, *Principia Mathematica*.

While the plague ravaged the cities of England, Isaac Newton began work on many of his greatest achievements. But little of what was started in those so-called miracle years was completed by the time he returned to Cambridge in the spring of 1667. Newton was tackling the hardest questions known to man, and in some cases it would be years before he solved them.

CHAPTER FOUR
MASTER AND FELLOW

On September 2, 1666, the Great Fire of London consumed over 436 acres, thirteen thousand houses, and eighty-seven churches in what was by then Europe's largest city. Seventy-five percent of the old walled city was destroyed, including St. Paul's Cathedral. Thousands were left homeless and destitute. To a population already devastated by plague, this disaster seemed a judgment from God.

That same fall Cambridge University reopened its doors. Isaac returned there in March 1667, to work on his master's degree. He needed a fellowship in order to meet financial commitments, but there were only nine positions available to sixty applicants. He had to undergo rigorous examinations to compete for one of the

The Great Fire followed quickly on the Plague's heels, destroying much of central London in the fall of 1666.

highly sought positions. On October 2, 1667, Isaac Newton was made a fellow at Trinity College. He had to take a vow promising that he would "embrace the true religion of Christ with all my soul and also that I will either set Theology as the object of my studies and will take holy orders when the time prescribed by these statutes arrives, or I will resign from the college."

In keeping with the fellowship agreement, Newton received a yearly stipend, plus an allowance to buy his scholar's robes. When he completed his degree, the stipend would increase, as would his livery allowance. He was also given free living quarters. In addition to his stipend, he had income from some rental properties he had inherited and an annual allowance from his mother.

His financial situation had improved somewhat in the years since he first arrived in Cambridge as a subsizar.

In March 1668, Isaac Newton received his MA degree and became a fellow. For a few days he let himself relax. He even visited some taverns. He redecorated his rooms—crimson was the dominant color—and bought some new clothes. He also made his first visit to London. Newton left Trinity on August 5, 1668, and returned in late September. There is no record of how he passed the time in the capital city, but he did spend almost ten pounds in less than two months—the same amount he had been able to make last an entire year.

Back at Trinity, Newton soon withdrew into his work again. He lived the majority of his life isolated from the daily affairs that filled most people's days. Maybe it was because of the emotional blows he suffered as a child, or the demands made by his own insatiable and nearly overpowering genius, but whatever the reason, Newton always seemed happiest alone.

Humphrey Newton (a secretary of Isaac's in the 1680s and no relation to the scientist) later recalled, "He always kept close to his studies" and "very rarely went a visiting." He no longer went to the pub or bowled or rode, taking no exercise at all so he could devote himself wholly to his research. In his daily life he was still as absentminded and forgetful as he had been on the farm. Newton did not eat very well, and seemed not to care at all about his appearance. Often he forgot to eat. Humphrey Newton related his dining habits: "He very rarely went to Dine in the Hall unless upon some Publick Dayes, and then, if He has not been minded, would go very carelessly, with Shooes down at Heels, Stockins unty'd, surplice on, and his Head scarcely comb'd."

Newton's reputation for forgetfulness and a slovenly appearance was gradually superseded by the growing awareness of his genius. Sometimes when walking, he would sketch an idea in the gravel, drawing diagrams and scratching out mathematical symbols. When the other Trinity fellows came upon the drawings they always walked around them out of respect for the scholar's eccentric mind.

In 1668, Danish mathematician Nicholas Mercator (c.1620-1687) published his great work, *Logarithmotechnia (The Art of Logarithms)*. John Collins, a Royal Society member and an amateur mathematician who corresponded with a great many others, acquired a copy of Mercator's book and sent it to his acquaintance, Professor Isaac Barrow. Barrow was the first Lucasian Professor of Mathematics at Cambridge University and, as Newton's teacher, had recognized his mathematical genius right away. Barrow quickly passed the manuscript on to Isaac Newton, now his young colleague.

Logarithmotechnia presented a new method of calculating logarithms. After studying the text, Newton wrote a short response called *De Analysi per Aequationes Infinitas* (On Analysis by Infinite Series), in which he detailed the work he had done with logarithms several years earlier, in Woolsthorpe. Newton sent his paper to

Barrow, who immediately realized its worth. He asked Isaac's permission to share it with Collins. Newton refused at first, but finally agreed so long as his anonymity was maintained. After more time passed, Barrow was able to persuade Isaac to present the manuscript to the Royal Society. However, Newton still refused to give him permission to publish it. Collins, meanwhile, made a copy for himself and sent copies to many well-known mathematicians of the day.

It was fortunate for Newton's career that, in spite of his apparent wishes to remain anonymous, he was developing a reputation for his brilliance. At the time, promotions at the university were granted based primarily on seniority. New faculty members had little hope of advancement, but young Newton was emerging as a man whose immense talents could not be denied. His connection with the senior fellow Humphrey Babington may have helped. In addition, Professor Barrow had become quite impressed with the young master's mathematical skills.

As the Lucasian Professor of Mathematics, Barrow occupied the

Professor Isaac Barrow. *(Courtesy of the National Portrait Gallery, London,)*

first chair at Cambridge dedicated solely to mathematics. The position, established five years earlier at the bequest of Henry Lucas, was generously endowed with an annual stipend of one hundred pounds. In October 1669, Professor Barrow resigned his position to become a chaplain at the court of King Charles II. He recommended that Newton be promoted to the Lucasian chair, and the recommendation was accepted. At age twenty-seven, Newton was awarded the most prestigious mathematical position in England.

There were a few specific duties connected to the post, including giving a lecture on some aspect of geometry, astronomy, geography, optics, statics, or other branch of mathematics once a week. Newton also had to place copies of these lectures in the university library. Technically, most undergraduates were required to attend. However, tutoring had largely replaced attendance at lectures as the primary method of instruction, and few students attended his talks. Newton initially attempted to carry out his official duties with vigor, even wearing a scarlet gown when he lectured. Humphrey Newton remembered, though, "so few went to hear Him, and fewer yet understood him, that often he did in a manner, for want of Hearers, read to the Walls." He usually lectured for thirty minutes, but for less than fifteen if no one showed up.

Newton's first series of lectures was on optics (the study of light), an area of primary concern at the time. Preparing these lectures helped him review and adjust his thinking regarding the light experiments he had performed during his *anni mirabiles*. In 1669, he wrote a paper in mathematics, "Enumeration of Cubics," but placed the manuscript in his desk for the next twenty years. He resumed work on his calculus in the winter of 1670-1671 and began a manuscript called "A Treatise on the Methods of Series and Fluxions," which drew on the work he had done in Woolsthorpe. Apparently, he never finished the paper. He traveled home to attend to his mother that spring, and when he returned to Cambridge he seemed unable to reignite his interest in mathematics.

CHAPTER FIVE
RAYS OF LIGHT

Galileo Galilei had made his astronomical discoveries with a refracting telescope, which was a tube with a large lens on one end that focused light onto a smaller lens at the other end. This instrument worked by refracting, or bending, light. When light is bent, it splits into the various colors of the light spectrum, creating a rainbow. The high level of color diffusion resulting from the refraction distorted the distant image and limited the telescope's effectiveness.

Several people had attempted to design a telescope that used a mirror, curved so it would capture all of light's wavelengths, to reflect the light without distortion. Newton too wanted to build a reflecting telescope but had no success. Then he read a book by the Scottish mathematician and astronomer James Gregory that explained a design he thought might work.

Newton spent many hours designing and building a special mirror for the telescope, using a metal alloy he smelted in his laboratory. He used a piece of metal as his base because it was more malleable than glass and much easier to shape by hand. After coating the metal reflector with his alloy, he polished it to maximize its reflective capabilities. He then assembled the telescope and fashioned a mounting device. Newton placed an additional mirror at an angle inside the tube. This second mirror would catch the reflected light and redirect it to the focusing lens, which was mounted on the side of the tube.

Besides providing a clearer image, free of the distorting color diffusion (known as chromatic aberration), the reflecting telescope was a much more efficient and powerful instrument. Newton estimated that a refracting telescope would have to be forty times as long in order to be as powerful. Initially, he made two instruments. He told his mathematician friend John Collins about his design, and Collins notified the Royal Society about the invention. Late in 1671, the Society asked to see it.

Newton entrusted one of the telescopes to Isaac Barrow to take to London. When Barrow presented it to the Royal Society, the members were delighted. The amazing device was shown around London to many influential people, including King Charles II. Henry Oldenburg, the secretary of the Royal Society, wrote a

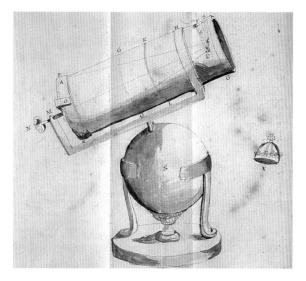

A drawing of Isaac Newton's reflecting telescope from his *Correspondence.* *(Courtesy of the Royal Society, London.)*

letter to the Dutch scientist Christiaan Huygens (1629-95) in the Netherlands, announcing the invention. As a result of his successful construction of the world's first working reflecting telescope, Newton was nominated to become a fellow of the Royal Society. He was elected on January 11, 1672.

In addition to constructing the telescope, Newton had also mentioned to Oldenburg that he had developed a new understanding of optics. The Secretary of the Society urged him to immediately forward a paper explaining his research. Although he procrastinated for a short while, Newton finally sent an account of his experiments with light to the Royal Society on February 6, 1672.

Newton's theories about the nature of light arose from the investigations he had begun during the *annus mirabilis.* He knew from his readings that Descartes had mathematically measured the degree of refraction of a light beam passing through a prism. Descartes, however, thought the color spectrum was *not* inherent in white light. Descartes and most other natural philosophers thought that color diffusion was caused by the medium (such as a prism) that the single ray of white light passed through. Therefore, Descartes had only measured a single degree of refraction, because light was thought to be a single ray of one wavelength.

Newton tested Descartes's theory with a set of experiments. He began by setting up prisms to break light into the spectrum. While earlier experimenters had only allowed the light to travel a short distance after passing through the prism, Newton placed a prism so that it intercepted a small circle of light passing through a hole in his window shutter and then refracted the light onto the opposite wall, twenty feet away.

If Descartes was right and light was a single ray, a small circle should be refracted onto the far wall. However, the spectrum on Newton's wall was not circular, but roughly rectangular, and was larger than Descartes's measurements said it would be. This was an impossible result if light was homogeneous—a single ray of white light. Newton then set up dual prisms and got the same result. Furthermore, the red wave of the light beam remained red after traveling through the second prism, blue remained blue, and so on. The colors of the spectrum remained unchanged by the second prism. If color diffusion was created by the intervening medium, the prism, then the colors should change when the beam of light passed from one prism to the next. The color spectrum could not be the result of the intervening medium, then, but a feature of the light itself.

Newton drew two conclusions from these experiments. The first was that light was not a single color composed of one wavelength. Instead, every beam of white light was composed of different wavelengths that mix together to form white. The second conclusion was that each wavelength traveled at a different speed, which meant each wavelength was refracted at a slightly different angle. This was the reason that the image on the wall was not a circle. Newton determined that the blue light at one end of the spectrum was refracted more than the red light at the other end, with all of the other colors falling in between. Today, we know that the colors of white light—red, orange, yellow, green, blue, indigo, violet—are actually part of a much larger electromagnetic spectrum.

During these experiments, Newton also measured how much each of the seven colors refracted when passed through a material other than air, thereby refining Descartes's earlier measurement.

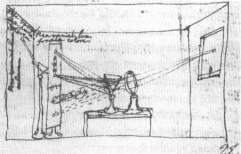

In perhaps his most crucial light experiment, Newton determined that white light was actually made up of seven pure colors. Here, a beam of white light passes through a prism, breaking into colors. The colored beam does not change as it passes through a second prism. *(From Newton's correspondence.)*

At the very end of his paper, Newton offered some thoughts about the nature of light's movement through space. The current theory was that light was a wave. Robert Hooke, a prominent member of the Royal Society, had embraced that concept in his book *Micrographia*. Hooke also advocated the homogeneous, or single ray, theory of light. Newton proposed that light might be a wave but that the wave was more like raindrops, or what he called corpuscles, than a single fluid stream. Newton's corpuscular hypothesis was just an idea, and he only mentioned it in summing up his theory of the heterogeneity of light. The main purpose of the experiments had been to prove that light was not homogeneous.

Newton's paper was read to the Royal Society early in February, 1672. Oldenburg wrote Newton that it had been well received and he requested permission to publish it. Robert Hooke took exception to Newton's conclusions, however, and composed a quick response that he sent to the Society on February 15. Newton's paper appeared in the Royal Society's *Philosophical Transactions* for February 19, 1672. The same day of the publication, Oldenburg forwarded Hooke's critique to Newton. Hooke claimed that he had attempted to duplicate Isaac's experiments but had achieved different results. In addition, he attacked Isaac's corpuscular theory, which he saw as a threat to his *Micrographia*.

Oldenburg continued to forward responses to Newton. Many commentators were open to, and excited, by his theories. Despite their accolades, Newton was deeply aggravated by Robert Hooke's response. Hooke had composed his comments rapidly, within a few hours of his initial reading of Newton's paper. (Later, Hooke would come to regret his haste.) Newton had spent eight years in research and performed difficult experiments before arriving at his conclusions, and now he had to defend himself against the attacks of an impulsive and insulted colleague.

Newton was so certain of his conclusions that he found Hooke's objections to be extremely frustrating. Furthermore, he was not interested in having to defend himself in an intellectual or scientific debate. He worked hard in nearly complete isolation and only released his discoveries once he was sure he was right. To him, Hooke's comments were "insufficient and sometimes unintelligible." Because Hooke complained more about the corpuscular theory than about the question of homogeneity, Newton thought that he had missed the point of the paper entirely.

Newton spent three months composing his response, which turned into a long paper, including large sections of what would later become a volume entitled *Opticks*. However, he delayed sending it to Oldenburg. March passed, then April, and his response to Hooke was still unsent. Oldenburg wrote Newton to caution him not to attack Hooke's personality in his response, only his ideas. Oldenburg was concerned about how Hooke, a powerful member of the Royal Society, would react.

Finally, Newton sent Oldenburg his reply to Hooke

on June 11. Instead of mailing the complete paper, Newton restrained himself to addressing only the issues that had been raised by Hooke. He rejected Old-enburg's advice, though, and used Hooke's name throughout. His anger at having to defend his work was evident. Having to defend himself in an intellectual controversy was a new experience he did not enjoy.

Another critique of Newton's paper came from a Dutch philosopher, Christiaan Huygens. Huygens would publish four increasingly skeptical responses to Newton's initial paper. At first, he saw Newton's theory as clever, calling him "very ingenious." In his second paper, Huygens referred to Newton's theory as being "very probable," but included some reservations. By his third paper he had decided that Newton had presented an unsound hypothesis. In his fourth critique, written in January 1673, Huygens totally rejected Newton's theory that light was composed of a multiplicity of colors. He had returned to the modification theory—

Christiann Huygens became increasingly critical of Newton's theory of light. *(Courtesy of the Library of Congress.)*

that the intervening medium, the prism, created the color spectrum and that light itself was made up of a single, white ray.

Newton became impatient, then angry, at having to repeatedly defend himself and his theories, which he believed without a doubt to be accurate. He finally told Oldenburg to end his membership in the Royal Society. Oldenburg, knowing the move would only give his doubters more sway, offered to waive his quarterly payments if he would stay on the membership list. Newton let the matter drop, but made it clear to Oldenburg that he did not want to be involved in any further philosophical discussions.

Newton finished his lectures on optics in the fall of 1672. A year later he began a series on algebra that continued for eleven years. His friend Barrow retired from London to Cambridge and became the master of Trinity College, a move that pleased Newton. In 1673, Newton moved into a permanent residence on the first floor of a building beside Trinity's famous great gate. He traveled to London at the end of August 1674 to take part in the Duke Monmouth's installation as the chancellor of Cambridge University. While in the city, he made no attempt to contact the Royal Society.

In the autumn of 1673, Oldenburg forwarded to Newton yet another criticism of his paper on light by a Jesuit scholar named Francis Hall, who taught at the English College in Liége. Newton, frustrated that his detractors couldn't seem to understand his work, composed a reply detailing how to proceed with his experiments. He requested that the Royal Society attempt to repeat the experiments at one of their meetings. In addition, Newton offered to send them another paper on light.

On December 7, 1674, Newton sent two reports: "Discourse of Observations" and "An Hypothesis explaining the Properties of Light discoursed of in my severall Papers." In his cover letter to Oldenburg, Newton stated his concern that the two papers could result in his having to "engage me in vain disputes." "An Hypothesis" was read at the Royal Society from December 9 to 16, 1674, and "Discourse of Observations" from January 20 to February 10, 1675. These two papers were larger in scope than his first paper on light had been, and they would reappear in his *Opticks* thirty years later.

The reading of the papers caused quite a stir among members of the Royal Society. As Newton had feared, new critics appeared and Oldenburg received more letters. Newton wrote to Oldenburg in exasperation, claiming, "I have made my self a slave to Philosophy." He began to look for a way to end all such future correspondence. He eventually stopped corresponding with Collins on mathematical matters and, when Oldenburg died in September 1677, Newton was at last able to extract himself from further wrangling with his critics. He was tired of arguing about light. He had been developing other interests over the last several years and now turned his attentions in new directions.

CHAPTER SIX
SECRET STUDIES

In the mid-1660s Newton began to read extensively about the art of alchemy, a medieval chemical science and speculative philosophy that aimed to transform comon metals into gold, as well as to discover a universal cure for disease and a way to prolong life indefinitely. Over the last five hundred years, from the twelfth century on, Europe had been the center of alchemical research. Because there was a constant fear among devotees that others might uncover their secrets, practitioners did their writings in secret codes. Perhaps Newton's love of secrecy and privacy drew him to this somewhat mystical field of science. As well, he must have found great appeal in the craftsman-like process of refining materials and the intellectual challenges involved in uncovering knowledge through experimentation.

Though its exact origins are not known, alchemy was practiced in ancient China, Egypt, and India, often in conjunction with astrology. The alchemist was in search of the so-called philosopher's stone, which was not an actual stone but a liquid, or elixir, which had secret powers. This elixir could be used to transform metals, but it could also transform people, making them immortal, or instilling other magical powers.

Instructions for the alchemical procedure were usually couched in vague, mystical language, in part to keep the uninitiated from having access to the experiments. Although alchemy eventually gave birth to modern chemistry, many religions considered it to be a heretical and evil practice. Alchemy was a threat to religion because, some believed, it usurped the role of a divine creator. It resembled magic, which was thought to be a tool of the devil. The alchemical procedure could also be quite dangerous. Some experimenters suffered poisoning from fumes, while other alchemists had their laboratories go up in flames.

As early as 1666, Newton began taking notes on types of furnaces and types of experiments related to alchemy. In 1669, in addition to buying two furnaces, he spent money on other alchemical ingredients and tools, including glasses, fine silver, antimony (a metalloid element used to make alloys), vinegar, spirit of wine, white lead, salt of tartar, and a six-volume collection of writings called *Theatrum Chemicum*. When he died, Newton's

Alchemists put their materials through a rigorous process of distillation, hoping they would end up with the elixir they called the Philosopher's Stone. *(From Vol. II of Bibliotheca Chemica Curiosa, Geneva, 1702.)*

library contained 175 books and pamphlets on alchemy and chemistry—one-tenth of his collection. Many were original handwritten manuscripts. Although he had stopped corresponding with others on optics and mathematical subjects, he apparently never stopped corresponding with other alchemists. For his alchemical writings, he used the pseudonym Jeova Sanctus Unus, Latin for One Holy God.

Newton was interested in alchemy as much for its establishment and application of general principles as for its secret, elaborate experiments. He was not the only scientist intrigued by the subject. Robert Boyle's alchemical research led to his discovery of the Boyle's Law, which states that a gas's pressure is in inverse relationship to its volume. Boyle was also one of the first to recognize the difference between an element and a compound.

In the late 1660s, Newton wrote two papers concerning alchemy. The second paper, usually referred to as "The Vegetation of Metals," was likely written around 1669. In it Newton said that the purpose of alchemy was to free the spirits from their fixed com-

The seven processes of alchemy as depicted in the first edition of *Ripley Scrowle,* 1588.

positions to achieve "metallick life & by degrees recover their pristine metalline forme." He also defended alchemy from critics who characterized its practitioners as greedy and foolish. Newton believed that alchemy was a noble pursuit with the potential to unlock the mysteries that confounded humankind:

> For Alchemy tradeth not with metalls as ignorant vulgars think. This Philosophy is not of that kind which tendeth to vanity and deceipt but rather to profit and to edification inducing first the knowledge of God and secondly the way to find out true medicines in the creatures so that the scope is to glorify God in his wonderful works, to teach a man how to live well, and to be charitably affected helping our neighbours.

Newton did not limit his research to alchemy. Even when he was most consumed with alchemical experiments, he was also absorbed in theological studies. He had inherited many books on theology from his stepfather. In addition, the requirements of his position at Trinity College meant that he was supposed to take holy orders at some point. His religious reading encompassed every major Christian theologian.

Newton applied the same methods of scientific inquiry to religion that he did to natural philosophy. As his studies continued, he began to question some of the most fundamental aspects of the Christian faith. He eventually became convinced that one of the core beliefs of the religion was wrong. The Doctrine of the Trinity, which had officially entered Christianity at the Council of Nicaea of 350 A.D., held that the three figures of God—God the Father, Jesus the Son, and the Holy Spirit—were one. Newton became convinced that the Bible did not support this belief that God was made up of three entities. He based this assertion in part on the First Commandment's dictate that there should only be one God. Clearly, Newton felt, the Council of Nicaea had erred when it adopted the belief in the Holy Trinity.

By rejecting the Trinity, Newton denied the divinity of Jesus Christ. Furthermore, he considered those who worshipped Jesus to be practicing idolatry. These ideas were heretical to both the Church of England and the

UNITARIANISM

The anti-Trinitarian beliefs of Isaac Newton were not unique to him. Unitarianism, the name given to the movement that replaced the belief in God as a trinity with the belief in God as a singular entity, began during the Protestant Reformation, a time when many religious teachings were being called into question. First rooted in Eastern Europe, Unitarianism gradually spread west, taking hold in England in the seventeenth and eighteenth centuries and spreading to America by the middle of the 1700s. Unitarian views became especially popular in New England. The first Unitarian church in America was established in Boston at King's Chapel in 1785. Poet and philosopher Ralph Waldo Emerson (1803-1882) further popularized the faith in the United States.

Unitarian teachings emphasize the role of reason and conscience in discovering religious truth. The Church expresses religious tolerance and a belief that the underlying goodness of all humans leads to universal salvation. In Unitarian beliefs, Jesus is seen as an extremely powerful, though altogether human, religious leader who is to be followed for his teachings and example, but not to be worshipped. He is not considered to be divine. Individual Unitarian congregations have the freedom to determine the religious views expressed by their ministers, which can be different from one congregation to another. Since there is no set doctrine, members have nearly total freedom of personal religious belief.

Catholic Church. Newton wisely kept his religious beliefs private. To openly proclaim his rejection of the Holy Trinity at that point in time would have destroyed him personally, academically, and politically. He did not even tell Wickins, his close personal assistant, who often helped in his alchemical experiments and transcribed many of Newton's other writings. Newton's characteristic isolation made him keep his feelings from even his closest confidant.

The ordination requirement at Trinity was one of the few actually enforced, and Newton searched for a way around it. Although he had supported the orthodox position earlier, by 1675 Newton could not bring himself to take an oath that included the doctrine of the Trinity. The only solution was to receive a royal dispensation from the king that would relieve him of the requirement.

This arrangement had been attempted previously in the case of another Trinity fellow named Francis Aston, who had several well-connected patrons. Aston's request was rejected in 1674, the year before Newton was scheduled to take ordination. For a while, Newton saw little chance of keeping his position at the college. He began to think of ways to make a living without the university stipend or the Lucasian professorship.

At the final hour, however, Newton was rescued. Although the details are not known for certain, the most likely story is that Humphrey Babington, who had sponsored Newton when he was accepted as a student at Trinity, and Professor Barrow once again interceded on his behalf. Barrow had influence with the king and understood better than most how important it was to keep Newton in his position at Trinity. He thought it was critical to the college's having a role in the future of mathematics and science. Newton's dispensation became official on April 27, 1675. He was now secure in his position and could pursue whatever scientific, philosophical, or mathematical interests he wished. Not only was Newton excused from taking holy orders, the Lucasian chair was itself released from the requirement from then on.

One of the reasons Babington wanted to keep Newton on the faculty was that there were some serious problems at Trinity. Enrollment had declined, which meant revenues from tuition had fallen off. At the same time, the school had committed itself to an extravagant library-building project. With about half the cost to be covered by contributions, the rest would have to be paid by the college. This meant reduced stipends for all of the fellows, although Newton's income from his Lucasian chair was secure. The library project dragged on for years, finally coming to completion in 1696.

Complicating the college's financial problems, Isaac Barrow, the master of Trinity and Newton's friend and mentor, died in 1677. The Reverend John North replaced him as master, but his reign did not go smoothly and before long the college united against him. North's successor did no better at stabilizing the college. In fact, he was notorious for being absent most of the time. Without strong leadership at a time when the college greatly needed it, the financial crisis at Trinity only got worse.

During these years Newton suffered several personal losses. In the spring of 1679, his mother became very ill with a malignant fever. The term malignant fever was a general diagnosis in the seventeenth century. Hannah Smith could have had any number of diseases. Over the course of his twelve years at Trinity, Newton had visited his mother only six times. This visit would be their last. Newton spent months nursing her. The skillful hands that had constructed the world's first reflecting telescope now tended his mother's bandages. She died on June 4, 1679.

After his mother's death, Newton remained in Woolsthorpe to settle her estate. The legal process took several months and kept him away from Trinity for almost three quarters of a year.

In 1683, Newton suffered another personal loss. His longtime associate and assistant John Wickins resigned his fellowship. Wickins had been mostly absent from campus for the last few years, only appearing a few weeks a year. Although he remained on the books as a fellow until the end of 1684, Wickins's last visit to Trinity was in March of 1683. He left to take a position as rector of a church in Stoke Edith, Hereford, where he married and began raising a family. A Wickins would occupy the rectory at Stoke Edith for at least the next century. Wickins's move was a blow to Newton, who, as usual, had few friends and even fewer confidants.

It was late in 1683, when Humphrey Newton came to work for Isaac. He worked as a secretary and took over many of the other tasks Wickins had performed—heavy lifting in the alchemy lab, overseeing experiments when Newton was otherwise engaged, and re-copying rough texts into readable manuscripts.

Throughout the decade of the 1680s, Newton spent a great deal of time on his theological and alchemical research. In 1685, King James II had assumed the throne following the death of Charles II. The new king began to implement policies that were favorable to Catholicism. Protestant resistance to his government was widespread. Newton was quite vocal in his denunciation of the Catholic faith.

One of the major works Newton composed during this period was "The Philosophical Origins of Gentile Theology." It deviated more from traditional religions than his earlier writings had. In this paper, Newton traced religious development since the great flood of the Old Testament. Newton proposed that Noah, his sons, and his grandchildren were the original gods

King James II practiced Catholicism, and many in England, including Sir Isaac Newton, feared he would convert the country to his faith. *(Courtesy of the National Portrait Gallery, London.)*

because they were the only survivors of the flood. After settling in Egypt, their religion was taught to all who came after them. Over time, all ancient people came to worship the same twelve gods, who were in fact the ancestors of Noah. As different cultures developed, these gods were replaced with the great kings and heroes of each individual culture. This process of creating a divinity from mortal human beings was, for Newton, an affront to true religion. Newton believed that Jesus was a great prophet along the lines of Moses but that he was not divine.

Newton wanted to find the one true God, who he felt was the ancestor of all other gods and the creator of the universe. He believed this Grand Deity could only be found in nature. He thought the geocentric model of the universe, which the Catholic Church had defended when it put Galileo on trial, was an example of how religion had degenerated over time. Placing the Earth at the center of the universe was just another example of human vanity supplanting the glory of God.

Newton never attempted to publish "The Philosophical Origins of Gentile Theology," and its existence was not discovered until the twentieth century. Most of the one and a half million words he wrote on theology were not read by anyone during his lifetime. Although Newton is known mainly for his great scientific writings, he actually wrote more on religion than on any other subject. The arguments and misunderstandings he endured as a result of publishing his scientific research were nothing compared to what would have happened had he gone public with his theological ideas. As he had so many times before, Newton kept his thoughts to himself.

CHAPTER SEVEN
PRINCIPIA MATHEMATICA

Newton was finally drawn out of his self-imposed isolation from other natural philosophers by a conversation that took place at a Royal Society meeting that he did not attend. In January 1684 young Edmond Halley, the architect Christopher Wren, and Newton's old nemesis Robert Hooke, were discussing the shape of planetary orbits. Years earlier, Johannes Kepler had determined that they were elliptical. Halley argued that elliptical orbits could be explained only if the force of attraction between a planet and the Sun decreased in inverse proportion to the square of the distance between them. Hooke claimed that he had already reached this conclusion and that he could demonstrate that all laws of celestial motion could be explained by use of this so-called inverse-square principle. Furthermore, he claimed he had already proven it to his satisfaction but intended to keep it secret until someone else reached the same conclusion.

Seven months later no one had yet presented mathematical proof that the inverse-square relationship described planetary motion. Halley decided to travel to Cambridge and pose the problem to Newton. At the time Halley was twenty-eight. He had served as an assistant to the first Astronomer Royal, John Flamsteed, who was gathering the most accurate observational data on the planets, the Moon and the stars ever yet assembled.

Newton and Halley had first met in 1682, following the appearance of a comet in the winter of 1680-1681. Many observers of the heavens believed that there were two comets traveling through the heavens. Royal Astronomer Flamsteed, however, insisted that the two comets were actually one. Newton had seen a copy of Flamsteed's theory and was intrigued enough to observe what was believed to be the second comet, first with the naked eye, next with a concave glass, then with a three-foot telescope, and finally with a seven-foot telescope. The older man's methods, and diligence, impressed the young Halley.

In August of 1684, Edmond Halley traveled to Cambridge in order to discuss his theory of planetary orbits with Newton. Although they had previously met, Halley was unsure how Newton would react to his visit and was pleased when he was welcomed graciously. They visited

Bodies in an Orbit"). He finally sent a copy of it to Halley in November 1684, and immediately began working on a revision. Although the document went through three versions, Newton soon realized he would need to do more investigation. What he was attempting was nothing less than to create the science of dynamics, or the study of the relationship between force and motion.

When he received the first draft of "On the Motion of Bodies in an Orbit," Halley instantly recognized its importance. It mathematically demonstrated that if the planets move in elliptical orbits, which was generally accepted as true, the inverse-square law had to be in effect. An excited Halley hurried back to Cambridge to ask Newton for permission to have the paper presented to the Royal Society and published. Newton gave his permission and on December 10, 1684 Halley rose from his seat and told the Society about his visit and the paper he had received in response.

Halley encouraged Newton to further expand his calculations, and in January 1685 Newton reported to Halley that, "Now I am upon this subject I would gladly know the bottom of it before I publish my papers." Then Newton withdrew into the most intense period of work since the plague years he had spent in Woolsthorpe, often even forgetting to eat and sleep. Newton devoted himself to this work from August 1684 to spring 1686, resulting in one of the most important and influential works on physics of all time, his great *Principia Mathematica*.

The *Principia* is made up of three books. The first

book begins by setting out three laws of motion. The first law states that a body continues in its current state, whether that is a state of rest or a state of uniform motion in a straight line, unless it is compelled to change its state by "forces impressed upon it." Newton borrowed this idea of inertia from Galileo but expanded its reach beyond Earth, applying it to all the bodies in the universe. Even the Moon, then, would continue to move in a straight line if not acted upon by the outside force of Earth's gravitational pull.

The second law explains why a planet moves in an elliptical rather than circular orbit. It states that the change in a body's motion is proportional to the amount of force impressed upon it, and the change in motion is made in a straight line in the direction from which the attractive force originates. According to Newton's first law, a planet has a natural tendency (inertia) to continue

---

NEWTON'S THREE LAWS OF MOTION:

1. **The law of inertia.** A body at rest will remain at rest and a body in motion will continue in the same direction and at the same speed unless acted upon by an external force.

2. **The law of acceleration.** A force F acting on a body gives it an acceleration **a**, which is in the direction of the force and has magnitude inversely proportional to the mass m of the body. This can be written out mathematically as **F=ma**.

3. **The law of action and reaction.** For every action, there is an equal and opposite reaction. Whenever a body exerts a force on another body, the second body exerts a force of equal magnitude and opposite direction on the first.

---

moving in a straight line and would keep going into outer space were there not some force keeping it from doing so. This tendency to keep moving along its course is counteracted by the Sun's attractive force, which Newton called centripetal force. Planets, then, are pulled toward the Sun at a right angle, in the direction of the impressed force, as the Moon is pulled toward Earth.

Newton's third law states, "To every action [or force] there is always opposed an equal reaction." If one object

CENTRIPETAL FORCE

When Newton understood that an object in motion at a constant speed will continue in a straight line unless impressed by another force, he made two determinations about an object in circular motion: First, the object must accelerate in order to maintain a constant speed, because it constantly changes direction. Second, it must be acted upon by an inward directed—centripetal—force. This force is a product of the acceleration. If, for instance, you twirl a ball on a string, the string transmits the centripetal force to the ball and forces it into a circular motion. In the planetary system the gravitational force of the Sun is the string that holds the planets in orbit.

exerts a force on a second object, the second object exerts an equal and opposite force on the first. Earth pulls the Moon; the Moon pulls Earth. The apple pulls Earth with the same force Earth pulls the apple, but the apple loses the battle because of Earth's larger mass, or what Newton called its greater "quantity of matter."

Every object in nature is subject to these same laws of motion. Nature, Newton said, is "exceedingly simple."

He asserted that the attractive force of gravity is not limited to planets, the Moon, or the Sun; it applies universally, to all bodies in nature, with its force dependent only on the body's "quantity of matter."

In Newton's world, all change is a change in motion. A resting object will remain at rest until a force sets it in motion. Once a body is in motion, it will remain in motion until another force returns it to rest. An object in motion will move in a straight line unless it is forced to change its direction by an "impressed force." An object can do only three things: rest, move in a straight line, or deviate from that straight line because of the action of a force.

These three laws are presented in Book One of *Principia* as the foundation for the rest of the work. Sections of the book are accessible to the general reader, but most of it is highly mathematical and difficult for even specialized readers to understand. Newton had created a new science of dynamics and developed a method to explain it. The result was a challenging book, to say the least. After *Principia* was published, and Newton was famous, a student who passed him on the street was overheard to say: "There goes the man that writ a book neither he nor anybody else understands."

A look at some of the problems Newton wrestled with gives an indication of how difficult the book had to be. Gravitation is a general force, he stated, not peculiar to any body or any part of a body. If the entire Earth exerts a gravitational force on the Moon, and the Moon pulls back, how much of each force comes from the center of the orbs and how much was spread across each surface as a whole? Newton and Hooke, among others, had wrestled with this problem for years. In the *Principia,* Newton was finally able to determine that the inverse-square law applied: a sphere attracts objects at a force inversely proportional to the square of the distance to its own center.

The final section of *Principia,* Book III is entitled *System of the World.* In it Newton addresses some of the questions about astronomy he had wrestled with for years and, in the process, uses the law of gravitation to "demonstrate the Frame of the System of the World." Using data gathered by Astronomer Royal John Flamsteed, Newton studied Earth's moon, which has a highly irregular orbit. He was unable to fully calculate how much of this irregularity was caused by Earth's gravity and how much by the Sun's, but he did determine that the rise and fall of the tides was due primarily to the Moon's gravitational pull. Newton's universe was held together by gravitational force. When he turned his attention to Ju-

Title page of Newton's *Principia Mathematica,* 1687. *(Photo Edward Leigh.)*

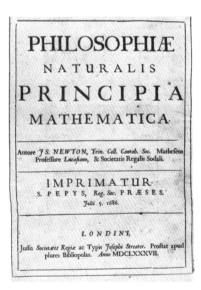

PHILOSOPHIÆ

NATURALIS

PRINCIPIA

MATHEMATICA.

Autore JS. NEWTON, Trin. Coll. Cantab. Soc. Matheseos Professore Lucasiano, & Societatis Regalis Sodali.

IMPRIMATUR
S. PEPYS, Reg. Soc. PRÆSES.
Julii 5. 1686.

LONDINI,

Jussu Societatis Regiæ ac Typis Josephi Streater. Prostat apud plures Bibliopolas. Anno MDCLXXXVII.

piter, Newton was able to calculate the gravitational attraction between the massive planet and its four known satellites. For the very first time it was understood that the same laws that applied to Earth also applied to the entire universe. This was a remarkable development in our understanding of the way the universe is organized.

Newton also derived measurements of the planets, and realized that they were not exact spheres but were flattened at the poles. This oblate shape was due to the bulge at the equator, a product of rotation. Because Earth is not a perfectly spherical body, its gravitational field is not constant. The gravitational pull of the Moon is stronger where the amount of matter is greatest, at the equator. The unequal force causes Earth's axis of rotation to wobble, which in turn causes the axis to change its angle over time. This change, known as precession, had been observed by the ancient Greeks but never fully understood. Newton calculated the precession as a conical motion and found that it takes approximately 26,000 years for Earth to complete a cone.

In addition to taming the planets, Newton offered an explanation for the movements of comets. His contemporaries believed comets followed no rules when they streaked across the heavens. Newton calculated that they moved within the Sun's gravitational field, and orbited in some type of ellipse more dramatic than that of a planet. Halley later seized on this theory and began calculating data to determine if comets return at regular intervals. He began his study with the comet of 1682 he had seen while traveling to Paris. Indeed this comet, which bears his name, returns every seventy-five years.

Newton's law of gravitation combined the disparate parts of the universe into one. The same force that explained Kepler's discoveries in planetary motion also described the results of Galileo's studies in falling bodies on Earth, and it could be described mathematically. The universe was absolute, rational, and unfeeling. This new science of motion joined astronomy and physics into one science of nature.

When Newton presented the first part of his *Principia* to the Royal Society it immediately created a sensation. With Halley working as its champion, the Society decided in May 1686 to take on the task of publishing it. However, it was soon discovered that the Royal Society's treasury was empty of funds. The members turned to Halley, who agreed to finance the publication out of his own pocket and to act as editor.

This was a gamble for Halley. He was a poor man with a family to support. But so strong was his belief in the work that he took on the two difficult jobs of financing the publication and editing the work for the press.

Soon after Book I was presented to the Royal Society, Robert Hooke claimed that he had actually discovered the inverse-square law six years before. Hooke complained that Newton had learned of the theory from him, and now falsely claimed it as his own discovery.

When he heard Hooke's accusation, Newton became furious and threatened to withdraw the book from pub-

The Royal Society was stirred into commotion over Newton's *Principia* and the revolutionary ideas it presented. This illustration is the frontispiece from a 1667 history of the Royal Society, and shows a bust of King Charles II accompanied by philosopher Francis Bacon (right) and the Society's first president, Lord Brouncker, with an array of scientific instruments in the background.

lication. Halley intervened, suggesting Newton include a brief reference to Hooke in the preface. Instead, although he had earlier mentioned Hooke in the manuscript, Newton went back and crossed out any reference to his rival. Eventually, Newton calmed down and admitted he owed Hooke credit in three areas. He finally included acknowledgments to Christopher Wren, Robert Hooke, and Edmond Halley, but he still refused to give Hooke credit for the inverse-square law. Hooke and Newton remained enemies until Hooke's death in 1703.

It is interesting to contrast Newton's reaction to this conflict to the earlier conflict in 1672 over his light theory. Then, he had retreated from public scrutiny and stopped communicating with the scholars in London. This time he met the attack head-on and did not withdraw.

Halley was the first to read the book as it went through several drafts. He considered it an honor to work toward publishing the *Principia,* but it put him squarely in the middle of Royal Society politics. On January 5, 1687, a committee was appointed to investigate his worthiness to continue as the Society's clerk. The exact reason for his review is unknown, although it is suspected that Robert Hooke and his supporters instigated it. In the end, the committee decided that Halley was fit to serve.

Working with the printers on a book as complex as the *Principia* proved to be a Herculean task. Halley had wanted to get the first edition out by June 21; however, it was July 5, 1687 before it was published. He sent Newton twenty copies to give to his associates around Cambridge.

Halley composed an "Ode to Newton" and inserted it at the beginning of the *Principia.* The poem's final line sufficiently conveys the younger man's feelings: "Nearer to the gods no mortal may approach." He made sure that a copy of the book made its way to the new king, James II.

Halley also published a positive review of the book in the Royal Society's *Philosophical Transactions*:

> This incomparable Author having at length been prevailed upon to appear in publick, has in this Treatise given a most notable instance of the extent of the powers of the Mind; and hast at once shewn whar are

the Principles of Natural Philosophy, and so far derived from them their consequences, that he seems to have exhausted his argument, and left little to be done by those that shall succeed him.

By the following year, Newton's name was recognizable to the general public. Reviews of *Principia* appeared in journals of natural philosophy in the Netherlands, France, and Germany, some praising the work, others criticizing it. Gottfried Wilhelm von Leibniz, the German philosopher and mathematician, expressed shock that Isaac had not tried to find the cause of gravity. Dutch natural philosopher Christiann Huygens called the theory of gravitation absurd. Neither man, however, challenged Newton's mathematical work. The English political philosopher John Locke, in exile at the time, hoped to get hold of a copy of the *Principia* to read for himself. Locke knew Huygens and asked him if he could trust the mathematical propositions. Huygens assured him that he could. Locke was so impressed with Newton's work that he later befriended him and wrote favorably about him in his *Essay on Human Understanding* (1690).

CHAPTER EIGHT
GLORIOUS REVOLUTION

While Newton was immersed in writing the *Principia,* England was in political turmoil. After ascending to the throne in 1685, King James II, a lifelong Catholic, took a series of steps that seemed designed to reunite the Anglican Church, or Church of England, with the Catholic Church. Anglicanism had at one time been closely aligned with Catholicism, acknowledging the pope's ultimate authority until the 1520s, when a dispute arose between the pope and Henry VIII. By 1532, the Church of England granted the monarchy total authority over religious matters, though England would shift back and forth between Anglicanism and Catholicism a few more times as monarchies came and went. But in Newton's time, many people in England were concerned about having a Catholic monarch, and the implications this would have for the Protestant nation.

One way James raised the standing of Catholics was to increase their power in the universities. While Catholics had been allowed to receive degrees, they were not allowed to become members of the faculty. In February 1687, James ordered that Sidney Sussex College of Cambridge give Alban Francis, a Benedictine monk, an MA degree and a teaching fellowship without his conversion to Anglicanism.

The king's action set off a firestorm on the campus and across the entire country. Newton joined other teachers in drafting a letter to one of the administrators at Cambridge University urging him to save the university from Catholic influence. They also published a pamphlet called "An Account of the Cambridge Case," written at least in part by Newton, which detailed the political and religious implications of the actions of the throne. Several members of the university senate sent letters protesting Francis's appointment, fearing that his would be the first of many. The defiant king sent a second mandate with a warning attached that any university administrators who opposed him did so at their own risk.

On March 11, 1687, the senate met to consider the second letter mandate. By this point, Newton had completed the *Principia,* so he had more time to commit to the cause. While it may seem uncharacteristic that the reticent Newton would come forward in this crisis, he

An imposing figure in politics as well as science, Newton often felt compelled to fight for his beliefs, even if doing so led to conflicts with his peers. He is depicted here at age fifty-nine. *(Painting by Sir Godfrey Kneller, 1702. Courtesy of the National Portrait Gallery, London.)*

was likely driven by two factors. First, he had little to lose. His Lucasian chair was secure. Second, he had a strong antipathy towards Catholicism and had feared the possibility of a Catholic takeover of Cambridge.

In April, angered by the negative response from Cambridge, the king demanded that representatives of the university appear before the Court of Ecclesiastical Commission, which had been formed in the sixteenth century to enforce the laws of the Reformation and the authority of the Anglican Church. Humphrey Babington and Isaac Newton were two of the eight elected to appear. They immediately began preparing for the hearing.

Just prior to the hearing, the faculty considered a compromise. Alban Francis could be granted his degree and fellowship, providing no other Catholic clergy would be forced on the university in the future. Newton argued vehemently against the compromise and the faculty rejected it.

The faculty delegation went before the Court of Ecclesiastical Commission four times in April and May. The Commission found the vice-chancellor of Cambridge University, who led the fight against the king, had committed "an act of great disobedience." He was removed from his office and suspended without income. The faculty delegation was furious at what they saw as the king's interference. It immediately put together a response to the king. Newton was very active in this fight—after he died five drafts of the delegates' response to the decision of the Ecclesiastical Commission were found among his papers.

The commission refused even to look at what the delegates had written. In the end, Alban Francis was denied his degree and his teaching fellowship. James II was furious, but soon distracted by other events. In 1688, the birth of James's son stirred up fear of a Catholic dynasty, and the Tories and the Whigs, the two main political parties, united against the king. Several English nobles offered support if William of Orange and his wife, Mary, the estranged Protestant daughter of the king, would come to England and depose James. William invaded with his army but violence proved unnecessary.

James, who realized he did not have enough support to win an armed conflict, fled to France. This bloodless overthrow of James II in 1688 became known as the Glorious Revolution.

In January 1689, representatives from all over England held the Convention Parliament in London. They officially declared the English throne vacant and named William and Mary as the new king and queen of England. Newton, who had held firm against King James II, was selected as one of two representatives from Cambridge. He left for London that January, where he spent the next year working on Parliamentary matters. In February, Parliament crowned the new king, William III, and queen, Mary II.

Once William was crowned, Parliament continued to work on developing a constitutional monarchy. This form of government sought to restrict royal powers and to install the Parliament at the center of political life. Religious freedom was granted all Christians, excluding Catholics and anyone opposed to the doctrine of the Trinity, ironically lumping Newton together with the Catholics he so opposed. Parliament also adopted a Bill of Rights, which would later be used as a model for the first ten amendments to the United States Constitution. The Bill of Rights, entitled "An Act Declaring the Rights and Liberties of the Subject and Settling the Succession of the Crown," allowed Englishmen to petition the government, granted them freedom from excessive criminal and civil fines and bails, stated a prohibition against cruel punishment, and forbade the raising of taxes without the consent of the Parliament, among other stated freedoms. Newton was curiously silent during most of the debating as the bill was being shaped, perhaps out of fear that his anti-Trinitarian views would become obvious.

While in London, Newton did much more than silently attend Parliamentary debates. His reputation as the author of the *Principia,* and his membership in the Royal Society, gave him entry into the highest level of intellectual society in London. He began, for the first time in his life, to meet and socialize with many new and influential friends. The great philosopher and political theorist John Locke had returned to England with Wil-

A seventeenth-century London coffeehouse. Newton frequently socialized with fellow scholars and philosophers in similar settings.

liam of Orange. His political writings helped to shape the new government and earned him a reputation as a crusader for liberty. He asked to meet Newton, having admired the *Principia,* and the two soon became friends. Charles Montague, also known as Lord Halifax, befriended the reticent scholar. Natural philosopher Christiaan Huygens was in London and sought out Newton for discussions on many topics.

Newton even discussed his religious views with Locke, and was relieved to find in him a sympathetic ear. They also shared a belief in the mystical science of alchemy. At one point, Newton consented to have his religious philosophy anonymously published by Locke, although at the last minute Newton stopped publication. This was probably for the best because the printer had discovered that Newton was the author of the heretical ideas. Had they been published, Newton would certainly have suffered great consequences.

This time in London seemed to agree with Newton. He let it be known that he was tired of being at the university and would be interested in holding a government position. Also, because Trinity College continued to suffer financial difficulties, it seemed like a good time for a career change. Newton tried to secure a position as provost of King's College at Cambridge. The current provost was dying, and Locke and Huygens believed Newton would be the perfect replacement. It seemed as though the position would easily be his. When Newton learned that the incoming provost must take

Nicolas Fatio de Duillier. *(Courtesy of Bibliothèque Publique et Universitaire, Geneva.)*

holy orders, something Newton refused to do, he returned to Trinity, disappointed but undaunted.

During this time, Newton accompanied Locke on a visit to a noble's estate in Essex. There he found Nicolas Fatio de Duillier, an accomplished twenty-five-year-old mathematician whom the Royal Society had just elected to its ranks. The two had met briefly before but this was the first time they had an extended conversation.

When he first came to England, Duillier believed in Descartes's mechanical philosophy, but he soon became convinced of Newton's theory of gravitation. Before long Fatio, as he was called, was interested in Newton's other pastimes—theology and alchemy. The two men developed a very close friendship.

Fatio was fascinated by Newton's genius. He considered him to be the greatest mathematician ever to have lived. Newton trusted his young friend with some of his most heretical religious writings. They often met in London to discuss and exchange papers. Fatio's admiration soon developed into an obsession. He was possessive of the older man and jealous of others who occupied Newton's time. Fatio faked illnesses to gain

Newton's favor and began to make strange claims. He once boasted that it was he who had discovered gravity and that Newton had only confirmed it.

Newton did not seem troubled by Fatio's actions. He returned to Cambridge and tried to resume his alchemical research but soon fell into what we would call a depression. The past few years of concentrated effort—finishing the *Principia,* arguing with his king, and keeping his religious views quiet—were taking their toll.

In September 1693, Newton wrote to his friend Samuel Pepys. Pepys had been the Royal Society's president during the time Edmond Halley was publishing the *Principia.* Newton's letter was rambling, disjointed, accusatory, and above all, factually incorrect. At one point Newton referred to the current king as King James, although he had been overthrown five years earlier. A few days later, John Locke also received a letter. This time Newton accused his friend of attempting to "embroil me with women." He also called Locke an atheist and railed at him for undermining his chances for career advancement.

Both men thought Newton had temporarily lost touch with reality. Locke waited two weeks before writing Newton, who replied to his concern with a somewhat sheepish apology:

> The last winter by sleeping too often by my fire I got an ill habit of sleeping and a distemper which this summer has been epidemical put me further out of

order, so that when I wrote to you I had not slept an hour a night for a fortnight together and for 5 nights together not a wink. I remember I wrote to you but what I said of your book I remember not.

One explanation that has been made for this incident is that Newton suffered mercury poisoning from his more than thirty years of alchemical experiments. However, he never exhibited the two symptoms most connected with mercury poisoning—tremors and tooth loss. He recovered quickly from the breakdown, which was never the case with mercury poisoning. Newton's physical and mental exhaustion is another possible explanation for his unusual behavior. His excuse about staying up too many nights in a row during his alchemy research was probably true. He might also have been upset because his close companion Fatio had just departed England following the death of his mother.

Whatever the cause, this breakdown marks a turning point in Newton's life. By 1693, his great life's work was already completed. He continued to work on challenging problems, but without the innovative leaps and insights he had earlier displayed. He spent most of the rest of his life revising earlier work, with the exception of some new work on lunar theory. His most productive years in science were behind him and now he was about to embark on a new life, in London, filled with international fame and wealth.

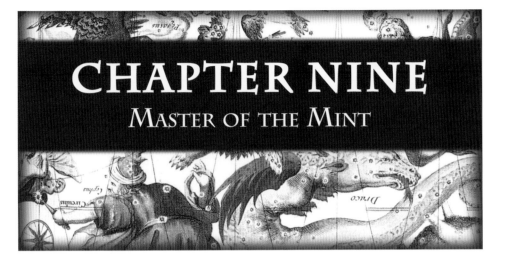

CHAPTER NINE
MASTER OF THE MINT

In September of 1695, Newton traveled to London with hopes of finally landing a government job. He had an ally in Charles Montague, who had considerable influence with the king. He spent two weeks in London before returning to Cambridge.

In March of 1696, Newton was summoned back to London to meet with the king. Although there is no existing account of his meeting with William III, it must have been successful. When he returned to Cambridge he began preparing to leave his home of thirty years. He filled trunks with manuscripts, correspondence, and books on such subjects as philosophy, physics, astronomy, theology, mathematics, alchemy, optics, and medicine. He left many possessions behind, including furniture and laboratory equipment, which eventually became part of an informal museum the college established after his departure.

Newton's new government position was as Warden of the Royal Mint, which had an annual salary of four hundred pounds. Right away, he made four times what he had earned in his distinguished position at Cambridge. In addition to the new salary, he continued to receive the stipend from the Lucasian chair, as well as rents from his lands in Woolsthorpe. Newton did not have to worry about money any longer.

The Royal Mint was located in the Tower of London, one of London's oldest structures. Located at the top of a hill on the north bank of the Thames River, the Tower of London is a massive castle of limestone walls and defensive towers, all surrounded by a moat. Past the dark

The Tower of London, situated on the River Thames, was home to Newton for many years. (*Engraving by Wenceslaus Hollar, mid-seventeenth century.*)

waters of the moat and the outer wall, a second inner wall, taller than the first and also ringed with towers, comprised the second line of defense for the ancient fortress. At the center was the keep, known as the White Tower, built after William the Conqueror invaded England in 1066. The White Tower had housed some of England's most famous prisoners, including Sir Thomas Moore, Sir Walter Raleigh, and the soon-to-be-beheaded wives of Henry VIII.

Newton's lodgings were also in the Tower of London, above the working areas of the mint. The Mint was in operation from 4:00 a.m. until midnight, and the atmosphere was chaotic and loud, with the clanging sound of coins being stamped out. Columns of smoke billowed from the forges. Soldiers, assigned the task of protecting the gold and silver, marched about. All of the machinery was driven by horses. Workers ran alongside them, scooping the manure and hauling it away. The mint spent almost 700 pounds in 1695 just to haul away manure.

Newton's appointment coincided with a massive recoinage of the nation's money supply. Counterfeiting had been a problem for some time, and the government feared a collapse of the treasury. The only way to stop such a catastrophe was to replace the old coins with new ones.

The former monarch, King Charles II, had instituted the production of coins by machine instead of by hand. When currency had been produced by hand there had been so much excess metal in each coin that it could be clipped from the edges and sold for a profit. It was impossible to clip machine-made coins. For a while, both hand-made and machine-made coins were in circulation, but people began to hoard the new coins because they had more weight. By the mid-1690s only about one in two hundred circulating coins was machine made, which meant the problem of clipping and counterfeiting continued.

At times, depending on supply, the gold and silver in the coin was worth more than the face value of the money. People began to melt down the coins into bullion, which could be sold abroad at a profit. During a period of inflation the value of silver coins decreased by more than twenty-five percent. Other countries would not accept English coins at their full value. When the government sought advice on what to do about the problem Newton had been one of the consultants. He wrote a pamphlet, "Concerning the Amendment of English Coins," in which he recommended recoinage, a devaluation of the currency, and using less silver. Most of the other consultants arrived at the same conclusion and the recoinage was already underway when Newton began his new job in April 1695.

The previous warden had rarely made an appearance at the Mint, and Newton's patron, Lord Montague, expected that he too would see the job as a gift that required little effort on his part. Newton, however, was not one to remain idle or shirk responsibilities. When he discovered that his boss, the Master of the Mint Thomas Neale, had little interest in the goings on at the Mint, Newton focused his attention on the recoinage. Officially he was the second man in charge, but very soon Newton was the "Master of the Mint" in every way except name.

In August 1696, Newton found a house away from the Tower, on Jermyn Street, where he would live for nearly ten years. Sometime around the end of that year, his niece, Catherine Barton, came to live with him at his new lodgings. Her father had died in 1693, leaving her mother, Newton's half-sister Hannah, nearly penniless. Newton helped the family by setting up an annuity (an allowance of sorts) for Hannah and her three children in 1695. When he invited his niece to come live with him, he likely did so for a number of reasons. Now that he was living in London, he needed a housekeeper and hostess. He was quite famous by this time and often had to host prominent foreign visitors who journeyed to meet him. One such visitor was the czar of Russia, Peter the Great, who visited him in 1697. The czar had an interest in scientific and technical matters. As a distinguished government offi-

Peter the Great, depicted in a 1722 tapestry, visited Newton in London. *(Courtesy of the Hermitage, Moscow.)*

cial, Newton also needed to hold dinner parties from time to time to help maneuver London's cutthroat political atmosphere.

As surprising as it may seem for a reclusive scientist to do so well in such a bustling, political position, Newton thrived at the mint. He got along well with Thomas Neale's two assistants, Thomas Hall and John Francis Fauquier, and his skill with numbers meant he quickly understood the accounting system. He studied each workman's job to make sure everyone worked efficiently and that no one was being overpaid. He worked closely, and well, with the city financiers. Many of his acquaintances in the Royal Society were amazed that Newton could move from the solitary life of a thinker and experimenter to an administrative position with such success.

Newton worked at overseeing England's recoinage with the same intensity he had shown his previous efforts. When London Tower opened every day at 4:00 a.m., three hundred laborers began work. Fifty horses turned the ten mills. Nine coin presses were in operation, each one striking fifty to fifty-five times a minute. In the summer of 1696, 100,000 pounds a week were struck, and by the end of that year, 21,500,000 pounds of new money had been coined. Newton supervised nearly every detail of this massive undertaking.

The salary scale at the Mint was set up primarily to benefit the Master of the Mint, who received a percentage payment for every coin made. During the recoinage, for example, Neale made around 22,000 pounds. At the same time, Newton was paid only his regular salary of four hundred pounds a year, although he was chiefly responsible for the success of the recoinage. Aware of this inequality, Newton quickly petitioned for a raise. His initial requests were not approved, but he was patient.

By the summer of 1698, the recoinage was complete. The Royal Mint recoined 6.8 million pounds in two and a half years, about twice the coinage of the previous thirty years. To support the recoinage, Parliament passed a law making counterfeiting an act of high treason punishable by death. Those who made tools for it faced the same penalty. Another of Newton's duties as the warden involved tracking down, arresting, and prosecuting counterfeiters.

Newton and his deputies ran secret operations to gather evidence against counterfeiters. They learned their way around all of the worst parts of London— socializing in the east end with tavern keepers and prostitutes, getting to know the thieves, beggars, muggers, and murderers who operated successfully there. Often, Newton and his men would disguise themselves and use false names. Newton was very successful at catching and prosecuting counterfeiters.

One of the offenders Newton went after was William Chaloner. Newton's memorandum to Parliament described Chaloner as "a japanner in clothes threadbare, ragged, and daubed with colors one quarter turned coiner and in a short time put on the habit of a gentleman." Chaloner had started out making useless tin watches and selling them on the street before falling in with other swindlers who pretended to be fortunetellers or doctors. After learning to enamel wood in the Japanese manner, Chaloner devised a way to apply enamel to metal and began to make counterfeit coins that easily passed for genuine.

Chaloner became something of a hero to certain portions of the London populace. He did not always cheat for money; sometimes he created elaborate practical jokes he called "funning." But even his practical jokes could have a nefarious purpose. One of his favorite schemes was to create a publication that attacked the government, then turn in the printers who had agreed to publish it and collect the government's reward.

Another part of Chaloner's appeal was his ability to evade punishment, even when he had been caught. At one point, Chaloner bribed all of the witnesses who were lined up to testify against him. Other times, he lied his way out of trouble, inventing huge elaborate falsehoods, a process he called "bubbling."

His ultimate "funning" was his proposal to Parliament that he become supervisor of the mint. He promised to improve it, but first, in order to demonstrate his methods, he needed to know the mint's edging secrets. This was such an obvious ploy to acquire new knowledge to improve his counterfeiting skills that Newton refused to cooperate. He accused Chaloner of being his number one counterfeiting suspect. Chaloner called Newton "that old dogg," which infuriated Newton so that he vowed to see Chaloner hanged.

Newton had Chaloner arrested and incarcerated at Newgate Prison. Then he bribed three prisoners to gain Chaloner's confidence and pump him for details of his criminal activities. Within three weeks, Chaloner was placed on trial for high treason, and Newton called his jailhouse informants to testify. Chaloner was found guilty and sentenced to death. The condemned man wrote Newton a long letter begging for mercy, but it did no good. On March 22, 1699, Chaloner was hanged to death in Hyde Park.

As dramatic as some aspects of his new life were, Newton lived the ordinary life of an English gentleman, full of comfort and wealth but without flamboyance. His favorite color was crimson, which he selected for draperies, hangings, bed and settee. He maintained a coach and servants—six at the time of his death. His niece, Catherine, ran the household and managed the servants. Some of their bills for goods and services survive. He paid for four landscape paintings to decorate with, as well as a set of twelve plates. He had an extensive set of silver: three dishes, three salvers, a coffeepot, two candlesticks, forty plates, and a full set of flatware. Complementing the silver were ten dozen glasses and six and a half dozen napkins.

Newton was usually temperate in his consumption of food and drink, but his parties could be quite extravagant. This was, in many ways, an era of excessive consumption. Newton mainly ate vegetables, only occasionally adding some meat to his diet, but a grocery bill survives that records the delivery of one goose, two turkeys, two rabbits, and one chicken within a week's time. His estate settled several debts for him, including bills to butchers, a poulterer, and a fishmonger, as well as a bill of nearly eight pounds for fifteen barrels of beer. It is impossible to know how much of this food and spirits was for private consumption and how much was used for entertaining.

Although London was full of diversions, Newton continued to do there what he had always done in his spare time—study. Once, Johann Bernoulli (1667-1748), a mathematician from Switzerland, sent a challenge in the form of a great puzzle to Leibniz, the German mathematician. Leibniz suggested Bernoulli send the puzzle to Newton as well, in a deliberate attempt to test the scientist's mind. According to niece Catherine: "When the problem in 1697 was sent by Bernoulli [Newton] was in the midst of the hurry of the great recoinage. He did not come home till four from the Tower, very much tired, but did not sleep till he had solved it . . . by four in the morning." He sent his solutions to the Royal Society and requested they be published anonymously in the Society's *Philosophical Transactions*. Of course, Bernoulli recognized the solutions as Newton's, remarking, "By the claw, the lion is revealed."

Newton received a great number of visitors at this

time, and Catherine was apparently the reason for many of them. She was, by all accounts, a beautiful woman who was also well-read, graceful, and a witty conversationalist—just the sort of woman Newton's political, scientific, and literary friends would be interested in. Charles Montague expressed a profound love for her, although their relationship never advanced beyond level of a deep friendship. The famed Irish satirist Jonathan Swift, author of *Gulliver's Travels*, was another admirer.

While at the Mint, Newton maintained contact with the Mathematics School at Christ's Hospital and was still a member of the Royal Society. His principal assistant was John Francis Fauquier, who served him for over twenty-five years. In addition to his duties at the mint, Newton occasionally served as a scientific consultant to the government. He judged a proposal for determining longitude given to him by the navy, for example, and the Royal Society occasionally called upon his expertise in mathematics and astronomy. In the spring of 1698, natural philosopher Jacques Cassini tried to arrange for Newton to receive a pension from Louis XIV of France. Newton declined the offer, however, because France was a Catholic country. In spite of that fact, one year later, Newton accepted his election into France's Academy of Science.

In 1698, Parliament passed the Suppression of Blasphemy and Profaneness Act, which would not allow any person who denied the Trinity to continue in public office. Laws, however, do not always prevent people from doing what they will. Richard Bentley, a minister and keeper of the king's libraries, held meetings in his quarters as often as two times a week of an exclusive club of Unitarians who rejected the Holy Trinity. He invited prominent men who shared his beliefs, including Christopher Wren, John Locke, and Isaac Newton. Had their views become public, their prominence could not have saved them from imprisonment or even death.

Newton's patience regarding his salary eventually paid off when, on Christmas Day, 1699, his fifty-seventh birthday, he was named the new Master of the Mint. Thomas Neale had been seriously ill for many months, and on December 23, 1699, he passed away. Newton had been quietly maneuvering behind the scenes to ascend to the position of Master once Neale was gone. Now, Newton would earn many thousands of pounds a year.

Newton remained Master until his death in March 1727. The years he spent at the Mint, much like his years of scientific pursuit, are characterized by an unflagging concern for accuracy and integrity along with a determined and industrious approach to every aspect of his work.

CHAPTER TEN
POLITICIAN AND PRESIDENT

After Newton became Master of the Mint, he resigned from his position at Cambridge. He had held on to his Lucasian chair and Trinity fellowship while in London for the past five years, long enough to be sure that his government position was secure. He officially resigned from the Lucasian chair in December 1701, and arranged for his friend William Whiston to be appointed as his replacement. Whiston was one of a few close friends who shared Newton's heretical religious views.

Around the time that Newton resigned his professorship, the university honored the departing professor by electing him again to become its representative in Parliament. Newton spent most of his time in the House of Commons sitting silently while the representatives argued over policy issues and financial matters. King William III died on May 7, 1702 and the new ruler, Queen Anne, dissolved the Parliament and called for new elections, as was the custom when the monarchy changed hands. In her closing speech at the Parliament's final meeting, the pious queen emphasized the role that compliance with the dictates of religious conformity should play in the upcoming elections.

In the election of 1701, Newton defeated a man named Anthony Hammond. Shortly thereafter, Hammond published a pamphlet entitled "Considerations upon Corrupt Elections of Members to serve in Parliament." Among other things, it suggested that radical religious heretics might overthrow the Anglican Church if they were elected to government posts. A similar pamphlet was published on the eve of the 1702 election, accusing many government officials of hypocrisy in their religious beliefs. Fear of having his Unitarian beliefs discovered might have been one reason Newton did not run for office again in 1702.

Beginning in May 1703, the facilities did not coin any new money for nine months. Free of his responsibilities at Cambridge and a good deal less occupied by the Mint, Newton began to renew his interest in the Royal Society. The organization had deteriorated somewhat from its heyday in the early 1670s. Its membership had dropped from more than two hundred members to fewer than one hundred, and few of these actually attended the meetings. The meetings themselves were not usually well planned and often had a sensational rather than purely scientific agenda.

From Newton's perspective, poor leadership was to blame for the Society's problems. His old nemesis and the group's former leader, Robert Hooke, had died in March 1703. At the next annual meeting, in November 1703, Isaac Newton was elected to serve as president of the Royal Society, although it was not a unanimous decision. Only twenty-two of approximately thirty members in attendance voted to allow him a seat on the council. Only twenty-four of the thirty voted to make him president. In succeeding elections, though he would be reelected, the vote would never be close to unanimous. Newton's years as a solitary scholar with little concern for whose feathers he ruffled had left their mark.

As he had done at the mint, Newton used his administrative talents and energy to reform the scientific organization. He regularly attended both the leadership council meetings and general society meetings, too. He worked to find a serious scientist who would arrange and set up experiments at the meetings, as Hooke had done in earlier years.

Even under Newton's leadership, the Royal Society did not give up sensationalism entirely. Dr. James Douglas, for example, performed public dissections and once brought in a dog with no mouth—a week later he brought in its skull. In 1709 "There was shewed four Piggs all Growing to One Another taken out of a Sow after she was killed." One participant brought in the penis of a possum. Newton himself once reported to the group that bran, if dampened and exposed to heat, would breed worms. In some ways the society continued to fall short of what it could have been. A man visiting the society in 1710 observed, "the president, Newton, is an old man, and too much occupied as Master of the Mint, with his own affairs, to trouble himself much about the Society." Nevertheless, membership returned to its highest levels and the organization's financial foundation improved.

In February 1704, Newton presented his last book, *Opticks*, to the Royal Society. It was mainly a collection of the papers on light that he had written over thirty years' time. Topics included his experiments separating white light into colors, his work with reflection and refraction, his study of the operation of the human eye, and his research with lenses. He explained how he had constructed the reflecting telescope. Also included were "A Treatise on the Quadrature of Curves" and "Enumerations of Lines of the Third Order," two mathematical texts. Even though the book was entitled *Opticks,* Newton included essays on the circulation of the blood, the workings of human metabolism and digestion, the creation of the world, Noah and the Great Flood, and the scientific method.

Opticks was written in English, which probably gave it wider public appeal than the *Principia,* with its complicated mathematical and Latin text, had enjoyed. John

OPTICKS:
OR, A
TREATISE
OF THE
REFLEXIONS, REFRACTIONS,
INFLEXIONS and COLOURS
OF
LIGHT.
by Sr. Isaac. ALSO Newton.
Two TREATISES
OF THE
SPECIES and MAGNITUDE
OF
Curvilinear Figures.

LONDON,
Printed for SAM. SMITH, and BENJ. WALFORD.
Printers to the Royal Society, at the Prince's Arms in
St. Paul's Church-yard. MDCCIV.

Newton's final book, *Opticks,* was presented to the Royal Society in 1704.

Locke, who had struggled to understand the earlier work, commented that he read all of the essays in *Opticks,* "acquainting myself with every thing in them." Abraham DeMoivre, one of Isaac's disciples, arranged for a Latin printing of the *Opticks.* The two men met at a coffee-house many evenings to discuss the translation and afterward, they would retire to Newton's home for philosophical discussions. Another disciple of Newton's, Samuel Clarke, actually made the Latin translation, which was published later in the same year.

The year after Isaac published the *Opticks*, in the spring of 1705, Lord Montague once again visited Newton. He convinced the well-known scientist to run for the House of Commons. During his campaign, Newton had to spend much of his time traveling between Cambridge and London. One such trip was in April 1705, when Queen Anne was visiting the university. On the sixteenth of that month, after much pomp and ceremony, the queen knighted him. He was now Sir Isaac Newton. She also mandated that the Lord Montague be granted a doctorate degree. The entire event had been arranged by Lord Montague as a way to create a political impact two short months before the election. The May election

The observation room at Greenwich, where Royal Astronomer Flamsteed studied and charted planetary and lunar motion. *(Courtesy of Royal Greenwich Observatory.)*

did not go as Lord Montague had hoped, though. Newton lost and would never run for office again.

Newton may not always have flourished in political battles, but he certainly did not shy away from conflicts that concerned his scientific work. John Flamsteed, who had been appointed England's first Astronomer Royal in 1675, had spent most of his life gathering data on lunar and planetary motions. When Newton returned to his mathematical and scientific work, he turned his attention to developing a comprehensive theory of lunar motion. This was a complex problem involving the interaction of the gravitational pull between the Sun, Earth and the Moon, otherwise known as the three body problem. Deciphering the Moon's movement became Newton's biggest challenge as he began work on a new edition of the *Principia*. He even told one correspondent that "his head never ached but with his studies of the Moon." Because his own observations were not nearly as comprehensive as the Royal Astronomer's, Newton's success depended on Flamsteed's sharing his detailed observations of the Moon's movement.

Newton and Flamsteed had long had a tense relationship. Newton had first attempted to solve the problem of lunar motion a decade earlier, in the summer of 1694. His calculations and models relied upon data provided by Flamsteed's office. Newton had trouble devising a workable theory and at one point blamed Flamsteed for his failure. Newton became convinced that the Astronomer Royal was unwilling to provide him with the data

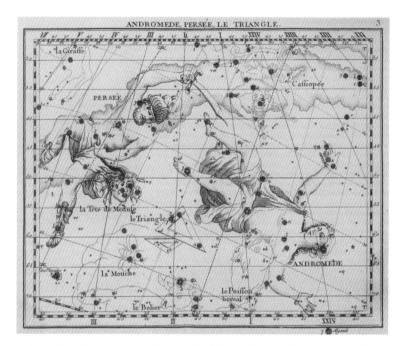

A decorative star map from Flamsteed's *British History of the Heavens.* His astronomical charts were crucial to Newton's studies of lunar motion.

he so needed. Flamsteed was indignant at this allegation.

When Newton returned to the problem again in April of 1704, after the publication of *Opticks,* he took the bold step of traveling by boat down the Thames River to visit Flamsteed at the Royal Observatory in Greenwich. His goal was to make sure he would have access to any of the observations he thought he might need in order to understand the motion of the moon. It became clear right away, however, that Flamsteed had no intention of placing Newton's needs before his own. Flamsteed was nearing completion of his life's work, *Historia coelestis* (*History of the Heavens*), which was to be the most complete catalog of stars ever produced. He hoped to have the Royal Society's help with its publication.

When Prince George offered to pay for publication of *Historia coelestis* Newton saw his opportunity. He had the prince made a member of the Society and then arranged for the group to encourage its publication. Because Flamsteed could not deny a prince's offer, he had no choice but to begin sending his manuscript and papers to the Royal Society for pre-publication review. Newton named himself head of a committee formed to examine Flamsteed's work, which gave him access to the data he needed for his own work.

When it became apparent to Flamsteed that Newton was only interested in publishing the sections of *Historia coelestis* that applied to his own work he began looking for ways to delay its publication. Thus began a struggle that would drag on for years. When the work was finally published in 1712, Flamsteed considered it to be an inadequate edition. In the meantime Newton had him ejected from the Royal Society for non-payment of dues. Years later, not long before he died, Flamsteed would finally have his complete masterwork printed. He then tracked down and burned all the copies of Newton's version that he was able to acquire.

The feud with Flamsteed does not reflect well on Newton. By this stage of his life, he clearly considered himself to be above practicing diplomacy or taking other people's desires into consideration, particularly if he thought those desires stood in the way of his own investigations. Isaac Newton had become a legendary figure, almost a deity of science, and he was not above using his power to get what he wanted, regardless of the consequences for others.

In the meantime, minor problems at the Mint came and went. In 1707, for instance, England and Scotland had signed a treaty to combine the two countries into a single union. The agreement specified that Scottish currency would be converted to English and much of the planning for this huge conversion fell on Newton and his associates. A political crisis developed at the Mint in May of 1708 when Craven Peyton was appointed the new warden. Peyton, a member of the Tories, and Newton, a Whig, did not get along at all, and within a few years the master and warden were openly at war. Newton's political opponents, the Tories, tried to force him out of his position but he refused to step down. After Queen Anne's death in 1714 and the political shifts that followed, Peyton no longer posed a threat.

Newton faced a similar political struggle at the Royal Society. He had attracted many foreign members to the organization. One tactic for improving its reputation was to invite wealthy aristocrats to become members. He also arranged for some dramatic and impressive demonstrations to be presented. There were those who did not like what they saw as his high-handed manner of administration. At one point eight of the twenty-one board members resigned as a show of their unhappiness.

Although at times authoritarian, Newton's leadership of the Royal Society saved the venerable institution and restored some of its reputation. Prominent visitors were seated in great leather armchairs near the president. Many of the visitors came to the meetings just to see the great scientist. One attendee left a description of a typical proceeding:

> Whilst he presided in the Royal Society, he executed that office with singular prudence, with a grace and dignity—conscious of what was due to so noble an Institution—what was expected from his character. There was no whispering, talking, nor loud laughter. If discussions arose in any sort, he said they tended to find out truth, but ought not to arise to any personality. Every thing was transacted with great attention and solemnity and decency; nor were any papers which seemed to border on religion treated without proper respect. Indeed his presence created a natural awe in the assembly; they appear'd truly without any levity or indecorum.

Throughout the years of his leadership, benefactors left healthy bequests to the Society that allowed it to prosper. Many varied topics of interest were brought up for discussion at the meetings, including the making of watches and clocks; the uses of barometers, thermometers, and magnets; the saltiness of the sea; how the eye works; and the parallax of Mars. Today the Royal Society continues to serve as a bastion of scientific inquiry and research.

CHAPTER ELEVEN
DEFENDING CALCULUS

Newton's lifelong obsession with secrecy eventually led to his most devastating conflict in a life that had no shortage of intellectual turmoil. The topic this time was Newton's greatest mathematical achievement, calculus. The question was one of priority: Was it Newton or the German Gottfried Wilhelm von Leibniz who had first invented the method?

Leibniz was certainly a worthy opponent. The son of a philosopher, he earned a doctorate in law in Germany. In his early adult years he lived and worked in Paris, Amsterdam, and London and devoted most of his time to science and mathematics. Beginning in 1676 he worked for a prominent family in the German state of Hanover, until his death in 1716. Today he is considered to be one of the founders of modern science and philosophy.

Leibniz first worked out his method of calculus in 1675, independent of the work Newton had done almost a decade earlier while staying in Woolsthorpe during the plague years. But Newton had refused to release his method to the world. Without Newton's knowledge, Leibniz had been allowed, while visiting London, to see material from the mathematical letters and papers Newton had sent to John Collins that detailed his work with the fluxions method. While historians have determined that Leibniz only received a sampling of Newton's work, this act of indiscretion would later come back to haunt Leibniz. In 1676, Newton wrote two letters to Leibniz. One of the letters provided Leibniz with many of the results of Newton's calculations without providing his methods, and in a second letter Newton politely stated his belief that Leibniz had stolen his methods and claimed them as his own. Both Leibniz's access to Newton's correspondence with Collins and the letters Newton and Leibniz exchanged would factor into the conflict.

Leibniz began to publish on his calculus in 1684 without mentioning either Newton's letters to him or the material that Collins had provided him in London. Newton made no public response to Leibniz's publications, but in 1691 he began working on a paper, "On the Quadrature of Curves," that was intended in part to establish that he had arrived at the method first. This paper was not published until years later, however, when it appeared in a shorter version as an appendix in *Opticks*. The controversy continued to eat at Newton for years, and he made reference to it periodically.

Gottfried Wilhelm von Leibniz and Isaac Newton feuded for years over who first invented calculus.

The tense situation between the two men remained an uneasy stalemate until, in 1699, Leibniz published two mathematical papers. In these papers Leibniz implied that Newton had borrowed his method, rather than the other way around. Essentially, the German was claiming that he had discovered calculus first.

When Newton attached "On the Quadrature of Curves" and another mathematical paper to the end of *Opticks* he struck back by claiming Leibniz had taken his work from the letters Newton had written to Collins in 1676.

Newton also released all of his correspondence, which he said clearly established his priority. Leibniz then wrote an anonymous review of the papers in which he accused Newton of stealing his work and merely changing the notations.

For years the controversy brewed. Then, in 1711, Liebniz wrote an open letter to the Royal Society insisting they create a commission to determine who should get credit for creating calculus first. This was not a smart move. Newton had, by this time, assumed almost total control of the Society. Behind the scenes, Newton hand-picked the commission members. In April 1712, one month after it had been formed, the committee released its report. The report had been written by Newton and, not surprisingly, it gave him priority for the invention of calculus. A later investigation confirmed that Newton had invented his method between 1665 and 1666 and that ten years later Leibniz invented his more complicated differential calculus.

Today, most historians recognize that Newton developed his fluxions first, and that Leibniz developed his own methods without borrowing from Newton. That Leibniz's method has survived these centuries is perhaps due to the fact that he was not concerned with secrecy, as Newton was, but seemed enthusiastic about communicating his mathematical discoveries. Newton's notations were difficult and coded, out of fear that someone else would discover them, make sense of them, and claim them as their own. Leibniz developed a system

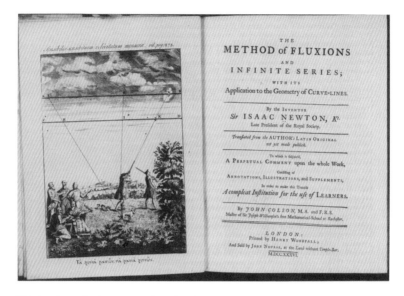

This book on fluxions was written by Newton in 1671, but was so mathematically complicated that it was not published until 1736, after much editing by John Collins.

of notation characterized by such clarity that it is still in use today.

In March 1713, the second edition of the *Principia* was sent to the printer. There was no mention of Leibniz's name in the preface. In June 1713, the printing overseer wrote Newton: "At last Your book is happily brought forth; and I thank you anew that you did me the honour to be its conveyor to the world." When it came out, the French writer and philosopher Voltaire remarked, "In London, very few people read Descartes, whose works have become quite useless; neither do men read Newton, because one must be very learned to understand him." Despite its difficulty, though, the book was in demand. Seven hundred copies were printed, and by the end of 1715, only seventy-one copies remained unsold.

Between 1705 and 1710, Newton had returned to theological work. Religion would remain a focus until the end of his life. In 1728, the year after his death, Newton's *Chronology of Ancient Kingdoms Amended* was published, and his *Observations upon the Prophecies* was published in 1733. These two volumes were more tempered than Newton's earlier religious writings had been, but that is in part because of his ongoing secretiveness. Newton spent the last years of his life readying his religious writings for publication by taking out any views that might be considered controversial.

Near the end of his life, Newton became a prominent man in religious affairs. He was one of the commissioners appointed to implement an act passed by Parliament that provided funds to build fifty new churches in London. He also supported the reconstruction of St. Paul's Cathedral, as it had sustained significant damage during the Great Fire of 1666. Although some of his friends and followers in the Unitarian movement published their controversial views, the extent of Newton's private heresy regarding the Trinity was not discovered until the twentieth century.

In August 1717, Newton's niece, Catherine Barton, married John Conduitt, a young man from a wealthy family. She was thirty-eight; he was twenty-nine. The couple had one daughter, Catherine, two years after marrying. Conduitt greatly admired Newton and began to gather material for a biography that he would never complete. His notes, however, have survived, and they describe a studious man who continued to pursue his ideas until the end of his life.

Isaac Newton met a London doctor, William Stukeley, early in 1718. Stukeley joined the Royal Society and the two became friends. Like Conduitt, he began collecting information on Newton. Both Newton and Stukeley hailed from Lincolnshire County. Stukeley observed in Newton a plumpness and "a very piercing eye," that he had a full head of white hair with no baldness, and that he had lost only one tooth. The elder Newton was serious and quiet, very studious, rarely laughed, and nearly always had a book and pen in hand.

Toward the end of his life, Newton's meals varied little. His breakfasts included bread, butter, tea, and boiled orange peel. He had wine at dinner but otherwise he drank mostly water. Newton would not eat rabbit because they were killed by strangulation, and he refused black pudding because it contained blood, which he felt made men violent. In part due to failing health as he aged, Newton mainly ate hearty amounts of fruits, vegetables, and broths.

King George II and his wife, the former Princess Caroline, spent many hours at a time with Newton in his later years. Initially, their discussions centered on how Princess Caroline might educate her children, but they gradually turned to philosophical and religious questions. When Newton mentioned that he had been working on an ancient chronology, she asked to see the manuscript. He did not want her to see it since it would reveal his heretical views. He stalled for time, saying his papers were out of order, until he could create a controversy-free version.

In the last twenty-five years of his life, Newton had his portrait painted at the rate of at least once every four years, much more frequently than the average citizen. This urge to have his image reproduced again and again suggests Newton's near-obsessive desire to leave behind physical evidence of his existence. Newton also began looking after relatives financially in his later years, often doing the same for acquaintances and sometimes strangers. He went to family weddings, often giving large sums of money to the women and arranging for future business with the men. Though he probably gave away more than average, he did reserve plenty of money for himself.

As Newton aged his health began to fail. In 1722 and 1723 he battled illness. Kidney stones made him give up riding in a carriage and entertaining. In January 1725 he developed a violent cough and his lungs became severely inflamed. He found it difficult to chair Royal Society meetings.

Newton's memory began to dim. He did not attend meetings of the Royal Society as frequently or guide them as smoothly as he had in previous years. Likewise, the council meetings were no longer run as well. The Mint continued to run the same as ever because of its bureaucratic structure. After 1725, Isaac rarely went there any longer, and John Conduitt took over his duties.

On a Sunday night in March 1725, having recovered from the lung ailment and an attack of gout, Newton felt well enough to offer Stukeley a vision of sorts, saying that our galaxy "is but a sort of picture of the Universe. God always created new worlds, always creates new worlds, new systems, to multiply the infinitude of his beneficiarys, and extend all happiness beyond all compass and imagination."

Newton's health continued to be problematic. Catherine and John Conduitt convinced him to take a house in Kensington, where they felt the clear air would do him good. He still walked to church and continued to study and write. When offered rides to church, he would decline, saying, "Use legs and have legs."

At age eighty-two, Newton had constant visits from doctors. He began to dispose of his estate, burning several papers in the process. On March 2, 1727, he presided at the Royal Society for the last time and seemed in good form, smiling, having slept well the night before. But when his minister visited on March 4, he found Newton in pain and sweating profusely. At that time, in the presence of John and Catherine Conduitt, Isaac refused the sacrament of the church. Soon he took a turn for the worse. Doctors found that another stone had passed from his kidney to his bladder. In the following days he was in often in intense pain. Conduitt recalled, "Though the drops of sweat ran down his face, he never complained, or cried out, or shewed the least signs of peevishness or impatience, and during the short intervals from that violent torture, would smile, and talk with his usual cheerfulness." On March 15, Newton seemed to improve, but by March 19 he was in a coma. He died early on March 20, between one and two o'clock in the morning.

Despite his earlier plans to dispose of his estate, Isaac Newton left no will. Conduitt claimed that the absence of a will was at least in part due to his generous nature: "He was generous and charitable without bounds, he used to say, that they who gave away nothing till they died, never gave."

Sir Isaac Newton's body lay in state March 28 in

Monument to Sir Isaac Newton in Westminster Abbey. *(Carved in 1731 by Michael Rysbrack.)*

Jerusalem Chamber, Westminster Abbey. He was interred in the nave. The Latin inscription on the monument ends with, "Let Mortals rejoice That there has existed such and so great an Ornament to the Human Race."

It was not only Newton's understanding of light, or the law of gravitation, that made him the leading figure of early modern science. Almost equally important was his refusal to speculate on the origin of gravity. By focusing instead on analyzing this force, Newton began the process of separating the scientist from the philosopher. Newton's basic principles of investigation have persisted throughout the modern era. They form the foundation on which today's technological civilization rests. For these reasons, Newton is generally considered to be the single most important contributor to the development of modern science.

TIMELINE

1642   Galileo Galilei dies; Isaac Newton born at Woolsthorpe.

1661   Newton begins student years at Trinity College, Cambridge University.

1665   Earns bachelor's degree.

1666   *Anni Mirabiles.* The Great Plague forces Newton back to Woolsthorpe, where he carries out important work in mathematics, optics, and physics.

1668   Earns master's degree.

1669   Becomes Lucasian Professor of Mathematics, Cambridge.

1671   Presents reflecting telescope to Royal Society.

1672   Sends first treatise on light to Royal Society.

1674   Sends second treatise on light to Royal Society.

1684   Edmond Halley meets with Newton at Cambridge; Newton starts work on the *Principia.*

1687   The *Principia* is published.

1689   Newton elected to Parliament as representative of Cambridge University.

1693   Difficult period some interpret as breakdown.

1696   Moves to London; appointed warden of the Royal Mint.

1699   Appointed Master of the Mint.

1701   Elected to Parliament as representative of Cambridge University.

1703   Elected president of Royal Society.

1704   *Opticks* published.

1705   Knighted by Queen Anne.

1713   Second edition of the *Principia* is published.

1717   Second edition of the *Opticks* is published.

1727   Dies at Kensington in March.

SOURCES

CHAPTER ONE: "Left Behind"

p. 11, "I do not know..." Westfall, Richard S., *Never at Rest: A Biography of Isaac Newton* (Cambridge, UK: Cambridge University Press, 1980), 309.

p. 12, "so little likely to live . . ." Ibid., 7.

p. 16, "Threatening my..." White, Michael. *Isaac Newton: The Last Sorcerer* (Reading, MA: Addison-Wesley, 1997), 15-16.

p. 20, "drinking twice..." Ibid., 23.

p. 21, "Stealing cherry..." Westfall, *Never at Rest*, 58-59.

p. 22, "Refusing to go..." White, *Last Sorcerer*, 25.

p. 22, "for suffering his sheep..." Ibid., 26.

p. 23, "foolish..." Westfall, *Never at Rest*, 65.

CHAPTER TWO: "Trinity"

p. 26, "a social pariah..." Ibid., 72.

p. 34, "I am..." White, *Last Sorcerer*, 53.

p. 35, "My Father's Intimacy..." Westfall, *Never at Rest,* 74.

CHAPTER Three: "*Anni Mirabiles*"

p. 41, "was in the prime . . ." Berlinski, David. *Newton's Gift: How Sir Isaac Newton Unlocked the System of the*

World (New York: Simon and Schuster, 2000), 24.

p. 44, "I looked a very…" White, *Last Sorcerer*, 60-61.

p. 44, "I took a bodkin…" Ibid., 61.

p. 45, "Amidst other discourse . . ." Christianson, Gale E. *This Wild Abyss: The Story of the Men Who Made Modern Astronomy* (New York: The Free Press, 1978), 366.

CHAPTER FOUR: "Master and Fellow"

p. 50, "He always…" Westfall, *Never at Rest*, 191-192.

p. 53, "So few went…" Westfall, *Never at Rest*, 209.

CHAPTER FIVE: "Rays of Light"

p. 61, "insufficient…" Berlinski, *Newton's Gift*, 82.

CHAPTER SIX: "Secret Studies"

p. 69, "metallick life…" Westfall, *Never at Rest,* 306.

p. 69, "For Alchemy tradeth…" Ibid., 298

CHAPTER SEVEN: *"Principia Mathematica"*

p. 81, "Now I am upon this subject . . ." Gleick, James. *Isaac Newton* (New York: Pantheon Books, 2003), 124.

p. 84, "exceedingly simple" Ibid., 124.

p. 84, "There goes the man . . ." Westfall, *Never at Rest*, 468.

p. 90, "This incomparable author . . ." Westfall, *Never at Rest*, 469-470.

CHAPTER EIGHT: "Glorious Revolution"

p. 94, "an act of . . ." Ibid., 478.

p. 99, "embroil me with women" Gleick, *Isaac Newton*, 150.

p. 99, "The last winter . . ." Westfall, *Never at Rest*, 536-537.

CHAPTER NINE: "Master of the Mint"

p. 110, "When the problem . . ." Berlinski, *Newton's Gift*, 161.

CHAPTER TEN: "Politician and President"

p. 115, "There was shewed four . . ." Westfall, *Never at Rest*, 652.

p. 116, "The president, Newton, . . ." Westfall, *Never at Rest*, 693.

p. 117, "acquainting myself with . . ." Christianson, Gale E. *Isaac Newton and the Scientific Revolution* (Oxford, UK: Oxford University Press, 1996), 125.

p. 119, "his head never ached . . ." Westfall, *Never at Rest*, 544.

p. 123, "Whilst he presided . . ." Westfall, *Never at Rest*, 682.

CHAPTER ELEVEN: "Defending Calculus"

p. 128,s "At last your book . . ." Westfall, *Never at Rest*, 750.

p. 128, "In London . . ." Westfall, *Never at Rest*, 750.

p. 130, "a very piercing eye," Westfall, *Never at Rest*, 849.

p. 132, "is but a sort of picture . . ." Christianson, Gale E. *In the Presence of the Creator: Isaac Newton and His Times* (New York: Free Pr., 1984), 574.

p. 132, "Use legs . . ." Ibid., 574.

p. 132, "Through drops of sweat . . ." Ibid., 575.

p. 133, "He was generous . . ." Ibid., 571.

p. 134, "Let mortals . . ." Westfall, *Never at Rest,* 874.

BIBLIOGRAPHY

Berlinski, David. *Newton's Gift: How Isaac Newton Unlocked the System of the World.* New York: Simon and Schuster, 2000.

Boerst, William J. *Galileo Galilei and the Science of Motion.* Greensboro, NC: Morgan Reynolds Publishing, 2004.

Christianson, Gale E. *In the Presence of the Creator: Isaac Newton and His Times.* New York: Free Press, 1984.

———. *Isaac Newton and the Scientific Revolution.* Oxford, UK: Oxford University Press, 1996.

———. *This Wild Abyss: The Story of the Men Who Made Modern Astronomy.* New York: Free Press, 1978.

Gingerich, Owen. *The Eye of Heaven: Ptolemy, Copernicus, Kepler.* New York: American Institute of Physics, 1993.

Gleick, James. *Isaac Newton.* New York: Pantheon Books, 2003.

Kuhn, Thomas S. *The Copernican Revolution: Planetary Astronomy in the Development of Western Thought.* Cambridge, MA: Harvard University Press, 1985.

Manuel, Frank E. *A Portrait of Isaac Newton.* Cambridge, MA: Harvard University Press, 1968.

Westfall, Richard S. *Never at Rest: A Biography of Isaac Newton.* Cambridge, UK: Cambridge University Press, 1980.

White, Michael. *Isaac Newton: The Last Sorcerer.* Reading, MA: Addison-Wesley, 1997.

WEBSITES

The History of Mathematics at Trinity University, Dublin
http://www.maths.tcd.ie/pub/HistMath/People/Newton/

Science World: Wolfram Reasearch
http://scienceworld.wolfram.com/

The Newton Project at The Imperial College, London
http://www.newtonproject.ic.ac.uk/

The MacTutor History of Mathematics archive, University of St. Andrew's, Scotland
http://www-groups.dcs.st-and.ac.uk/~history/index.html

INDEX